James Graham

Labour of Love

D1414122

Bloomsbury Methuen Drama
An imprint of Bloomsbury Publishing Plc

B L O O M S B U R Y
LONDON · OXFORD · NEW YORK · NEW DELHI · SYDNEY

Bloomsbury Methuen Drama

An imprint of Bloomsbury Publishing Plc

Imprint previously known as Methuen Drama

50 Bedford Square	1385 Broadway
London	New York
WC1B 3DP	NY 10018
UK	USA

www.bloomsbury.com

Bloomsbury is a registered trade mark of Bloomsbury Publishing Plc

First published 2017
Reprinted 2017

© James Graham, 2017

British Library Cataloguing-in-Publication Data
A catalogue record for this book is available from the British Library.

ISBN: PB: 978-1-3500-6367-9
ePub: 978-1-3500-6369-3
ePDF: 978-1-3500-6368-6

Library of Congress Cataloging-in-Publication Data
A catalog record for this book is available from the Library of Congress.

Photography by Charlie Gray and Jay Brooks
Front cover design by AKA

Series: Modern Plays

Typeset by Mark Heslington Ltd, Scarborough, North Yorkshire
Printed and bound in Great Britain

Labour of Love by James Graham received its world premiere in London on 27 September 2017 at the Nöel Coward Theatre, produced by the Michael Grandage Company and Headlong.

Cast

David Lyons	**Martin Freeman**
Jean Whittaker	**Tamsin Greig**
Elizabeth Lyons	**Rachael Stirling**
Mr. Shen	**Kwong Loke**
Len Prior	**Dickon Tyrrell**
Margot Midler	**Susan Wokoma**

Understudies

David Lyons/Len Prior	**George Beach**
Jean Whittaker/Elizabeth Lyons	**Emma Bown**
Margot Midler/Ms Shen	**Tina Chiang**

Creative team

Director	Jeremy Herrin
Set and Costume Designer	Lee Newby
Lighting Designer	Neil Austin
Sound Designer	Paul Arditti
Video and Projection Designer	Duncan McLean
Wig and Hair Designer	Richard Mawbey

Labour of Love

Characters

Jean Whittaker, *a constituency agent*
David Lyons, *a Labour MP*
Elizabeth Lyons, *David's wife*
Len Prior, *a local councillor and party worker*
Margot Midler, *a constituent and party worker*
Mr. Shen, *a businessman investor*

The above can also play:

Constituents
Delivery Boy
Party Workers
Takeaway owner

Setting
The local constituency office of a Labour MP in North Nottinghamshire, in the twenty-seven year period between summer 1990 and spring 2017.

Act One

Scene One

June 9th, 2017. Early hours of the morning.

The constituency office of a Labour MP. A couple of desks, filing cabinets, campaign detritus. Maps of the constituency, posters of upcoming events, local services. An old flip chart with tonight's electoral tally. Laptops on the desks – not much in the way of paper and files.

A front door exits onto a high street. Another to a back room kitchenette, stairs leading to the first floor.

A TV screen with rolling news. It's the early hours following the General Election exit poll. Results coming in. 'A hung parliament.' 'Shock Labour gains.' 'Theresa May's gamble failed?'

Jean Whittaker *is on the phone, next to* **David Lyons**.

Jean   Oh for Fuck's Sake!

David   What? Shit, what, not good? Course it's not good, who shouts 'for fuck's sake' when it's something really good?

Jean (*to* **David**)   Numbers are different Again, Tories up on *us,* this time, 129.

David   Oh for – (*Punches the desk.*) – FUCK'S SAKE!

Jean (*on the phone*)   Hold on. (*To* **David**.) Returning Officer asking if we want a *second* recount or not.

David   Uh, tell him yes of course we do.

Jean   David says tell that twat yes course we do – I added the twat.

David (*pacing*)   Oh my – this . . . this is –

Jean (*listens briefly, then to* **David**)   Just the bundles or full recount? – Forget it (*On the phone.*), just the bundles for now. Go, call me back. (*Phone down.*)

David   We're up, then we're down, up, down; we're like Ken Clark's fucking cholesterol. (*At the TV, national news.*) What is Going On? Why are we about to – compared to everywhere else?

Jean (*pacing looking at her phone*)   I dunno, I don't know.

David   I've never seen anything – a result, like this, have you? I mean –

Jean   Well, '92, that was a bit – remember? That caught us all by surprise.

As he talks he might head into the kitchenette, to top up his coffee from a pot, and hers too.

David   Yeah, but that *over*-esti- . . . isn't that meant to be one of the sacred cows of British elections? Labour support is always, always over-estimated, and what, this time we've been *under* . . . and it's *them* losing seats, *us* gaining, everywhere except frigging *here?!* Is it personal, I mean is it me, bucking the trend? OK it's me, isn't it.

Jean (*iPhone*)   Oh tickle my tits! Alan in Mansfield. Confirmed, it's gone blue.

David (*sighs*)   Right next door. They really are at the gates now, well –

Jean (*going to a regional map on the wall, crossing it off*) Labour since 1923, Mansfield, mining town, so there you are.

David (*at the TV – a new result*)   And yet somehow we're taking Warwick and Leamington? Frigging ooh-lah-di-dah Battersea. But losing seats up here. (*At the map.*) Look, following the line of old coalfields – Derbyshire North East, gone; Mansfield, gone, Skinner's majority slashed. What's happening?

Jean   Well, what's happening is if you're Northern, you're getting butchered, it's like Game of fucking Thrones.

David (*at his phone*)   God, rest of the PLP are all – ecstatic. Like a celebration you're not invited to, like we've been left behind. Why?

Jean   . . . Well, because we *were* left behind. Weren't we. Here. That's why . . .

A moment. The TV news rolling. A landline phone on the desk rings now, **Jean** *answers it.*

Hello?

Oh fuck off, Cheryl. (*Puts the phone down. To* **David**.) Cheryl.

David   Not tonight, Jean, please, be nice, it's her / job at stake too, and –

Jean   I am nice. I'm always nice.

David   She'll only call me inste- . . . (*His iPhone rings.*) And, wow, see? As if by magic –

(*Answers his phone.*) Cheryl, hello, Jean says sorry.

Jean   I'm sorry!

David (*on the phone*)   See.

Jean (*quietly to herself*)   That I ever met you.

David (*on the phone*)   No we'll go back over when they announce, no point hanging around. I'll bell you from there. OK, chin up. (*Hangs up.*) She sounds upset.

Jean   Oh why, 'cause I told her to fuck off.

David   Because it's *over*.

Jean   We don't know that yet, daft apeth, they're recounting yours.

David   Re-recounting, and I'm being realistic.

Jean   Pessimistic.

David   No, just –

Jean Masochistic.

David That's – not even –

Jean Satanistic.

David What are you frigging – ?

Jean I dunno, I'm just saying words now, I think I'm going mad.

(*Answering her iPhone.*) We know, second recount, wind 'not blowing in our direction'.

No, look we've just had this from Cheryl a'nall, we're not coming over, cameras, don't want his gloomy face looking all gloomy do we, we're staying here until whatever happens, happens; let me know.

And oy, text me, no Whatsapping, I've left the group.

No, I've left the group! (*Hangs up.*)

Fucking thing, buzz buzzing in me pocket all the live long . . . feel like I'm being electric shocked. Right sod it, I'm drinking. (*Grabbing a wine bottle from the kitchenette, and corkscrew.*) I am Resorting To Drink, that's what this has done to me.

David Four in the morning? Rock 'n' roll. (*Pacing.*) Shit. *Shit.* I'm going to be the last one to announce, aren't I, just in time for all the frigging breakfast – . . .

Jean (*pouring him a glass*) Have one, go on just take it –

David No, I'll still have to make a – thing, either way; speech –

Jean Oh don't be soft, what's it matter now.

David (*taking it*) I'm gonna be this election's Portillo, aren't I? Chris Patten, the Ed Balls. Better start working on my pasodoble.

(*Leaning over to his laptop.*) Look, Jesus, this is . . . 'Biggest swing to Labour since 1945.' Who knew Jeremy Corbyn was actually Clement Attlee?

Jean   Yeah, but Attlee won his election, Corbyn did very well but he still lost.

David   Thought you'd be more –

Jean   What?

David   Dunno, smug, 'told you so'.

Jean   I didn't tell you so, I thought it was going to be the apocalypse, 1931 style, like everyone else, doesn't mean I didn't believe in him.

David   You made sense of ours yet, swing?

Jean (*with a pen at the chart*)   What, you ready for your post mortem?

David   You don't mind if I drink through the diagnosis, doctor? (*Pouring.*)

Jean (*writing figures*)   So at the . . . (*Hugging the board.*) oh, I've just realized how much I'm going to miss my board. Some of my best times, plotting away on this thing. Oh the 'thoughts', the 'thoughts' . . .

Anyway, last count, which could be wrong, but probably not, you're trailing the Tory by just 129 votes, down from a majority of 6,063 two years ago. Except, hilariously, you've gone 'up' in actual votes cast, by 1,295, so that's a swing *to* you of – oh Christ, do the maths, channel me Carol Vorderman, 0.5 per cent. *Except,* the Tories have gained 7,000-plus votes since last time, so we're up, *and* they're up. UKIP down to nowt, but they can't all've gone Tory otherwise the Tories would be further over the line, so weirdly some of UKIP must have come *back* to us from 2015, despite us knowing on the doorstep that a lot of *our* lot went Tory, so basically – basically, it's a swingers' party, I don't know who's sticking what where anymore, except that the whole thing looks more fucked than a Bradford hen do.

David So up is down, left is right, right is wrong, behold the new politics. Go on then, how long since this seat wasn't Labour? How historic is in fact my failure?

Jean I don't know.

David Yes you do, you're an encyclopedia.

Jean What, utterly redundant in the modern world?

No, I don't think it ever has *not* been, so there, feel better or was ignorance bliss?

Look, the Tories always get in eventually. Like a shitty fly; you waft it out a window, it buzzes back in through the door.

(*Back at the board.*) Oh, and our lovely 'Independent' candidate who joined the race –

David Traitor.

Jean – traitor, 'they' snaffled a couple thousand off you, so that could have made all the difference. Oh the irony, that it might be our old friend that put a Tory into this seat for the first time.

David . . . So you do think I'm going to lose, then. I am, aren't I.

Jean Yeah, I think you probably are, yes.

David Got one of your feelings? Might just be the wine, it's old, could be off.

Jean It's not the wine, it's the Tories, they're old, they're bloody 'off'.

Honestly, people round here, short memories or what? I blame the coalition; Lib Dems, I do, honestly, they helped, like, build the bridge, from us to the Tories, psychologically, made it less toxic to – it's – do you know what, my little gay nephew Matthew, he says there's some folk start off straight, but then work out they might be gay, and as part of the transition, they go bisexual for a bit. 'Bye for now' they call it.

David   Some people are actually just bisexual you know, Jean.

Jean   I know that, oy, one of my best friends Tessa Cartwell, she licks and sucks, and she's the happiest person I know.

I feel like I've lowered the tone, I'm sorry.

David   It's alright –

Jean   No, if we're going down, I want to go down with dignity.

David   Oh what's the point, if I did keep the seat anyway. Being in opposition, past seven years, austerity, cuts, having to watch, helplessly, from the . . .

(*Looking around the office.*) Twenty-seven years.

(. . . *And then, unexpectedly, he starts to wobble.*) Oh God . . .

He covers his face. **Jean** *watches . . . before tossing some stationery at him.*

Jean   Oy, stop being mardy.

David   Ow! I was having a moment!

Jean   Just think of all the things you *hate* about being an MP you won't miss.

David   . . . I – right now I can't think of any.

Jean   The local party –

David   Oh those arse wipes, no, I won't miss those. Always made me feel like an effing – outsider.

Jean   Oh that's just cause you've never looked or sounded like them, still.

David   Oh I know, my accent not 'ay up me duck, ecky thump' enough.

Jean   Oy you, watch it.

David   And . . . (*Looking around.*) . . . I don't know. Won't miss the 500 emails a day, about litter in the park, or the neighbours' trees. And then the other stuff, the serious, depressing stuff, going down the list, just thinking 'poor bastard, poor bastard, poor . . .' And the abuse, threats of violence, the worrying about you and the other staff, here, when I'm away –

Jean   Well that's why we've got the new security, isn't it, cameras, buzzers –

David   Even though they should, they bloody *should* be allowed to just walk in off the street, that's The Point, but it all . . . now it all feels like it's just got so . . . (*Sighs.*)

Jean (*beat, gesturing him*)   Alright look, come on, let's get it over with, a brief moment of affection.

David *relents and goes closer to her as she hugs him.*

Jean   I am sorry.

David   . . . Yeah, me too.

Jean (*sighs*)   Fuck me.

David   I'll do no such thing, it's just a hug, calm down.

Jean (*pushing him away*)   Oh you . . .

David   Except in an hour or so, I won't be your boss anymore.

(*Realising . . .*) Or anyone, here, they'll all lose their jobs, won't they. Oh God, the guilt . . .

Jean   Text from Sally at Regional Office – where are me readers? (*Holds the phone out.*) God, are my eyes getting worse or my arms getting shorter? Oh for – why do people use them cartoon face things. What's that one?

She imitates the emoticon with her own face – a long 'mouth open'.

Where it's like open mouth, with massive sideburns; what's that mean?

David (*looks*)   That's not sideburns, that's hands, like he's (*Demonstrates hands to his face.*), that's like – shock.

Jean   Reminds me of someone.

David   Can't remind you of someone, it's a cartoon blob, Jean.

Jean   Does. Never forget a face.

David   It's not a face, it – wait, why are Central Office sending you a shocked face. Jean?

Jean   It's nothing.

David   Jean.

Jean   What?

David   *Jean?*

Jean   Stop saying my name, I'm not fucking Beetlejuice!

David   Don't protect me; if it's bad just say.

Jean   Oy, have I ever protected you, ever? And no point in fretting over that which you cannot change.

David   Is that another Bikram slogan?

Jean   Actually I think that's AA.

David (*raises his glass*)   Awh well, cheers AA.

They clink glasses. **Jean** *at her laptop.*

Jean   Do you want to go on *Today* tomorrow, (*At her watch.*) well I suppose it *is* today now, isn't it. Today, today?

David   No. Maybe. Who with –? No, fuck it. I should stay up here. Say bye.

Jean They could send one of them radio cars, you wouldn't / have to –

David I'm alright.

Jean *closes her emails and gets into a somewhat extravagant yoga position.*

Jean This is my favourite one in Bikram, I forget what it's called, you do them in the same order every time so it doesn't matter, the names, but – this.

She prepares herself and gets into the position.

See, look at that, my age, as limber as a twenty-one year old, nearly. It's about 'discovery', Bikram. You 'discover' . . . this mind numbing pain in muscles you never knew were there.

(*Gets back up, yelling at some TV commentary.*) Yes we know, thank you! Stop rubbing salt on our chips! No, that's not right, salt on your chips is good, what do I –?

David Salt on your wound and/piss –

Jean Piss on your chips, yeah. Well – that.

David I should actually say something. Shouldn't I? My speech, if I'm going? A rallying cry; no, a 'warning', to the party, I mean . . . everyone's acting like we've won without winning. Which is hubristic, to say the least. I mean fuck me, when we go 'up' in university towns and cities for the same reasons we're 'down' round here. Lose the 'heartlands' for being too soft on immigration, lose the young metropolitans for being too hard. Too radical for the old, too safe for the young. Too soft-Brexit for Leavers, too hard for Remain. Too left, too right, too old, too new; do you know what they can celebrate all they fucking like, I have no actual clue where we bloody well go from here, I don't.

Jean 'Where do we go, what do we do?'

David Yeah well, I'm not sure I *do* give a damn, anymore; that's all we ever seem to do, this party, long as I can remember; soul-searching, introspection. How can we still not know, a hundred years on, who we fucking are and why . . .

Jean   Well, it's a movement, int'it, movements don't stop, they 'move'.

Time I moved on, number of years I've been surrounded by these walls, longer than you. Most of my life. This – this *was* my . . .

God, do you know, loyalty's not all it's cracked up to be, is it, loving just one thing. A person, a party, bloody hurts when it goes. Wish I was frigging bisexual, foot in any camp, sounds fun.

David   Bisexual doesn't mean you're metrosexual.

Jean   What's metrosexual got to do with it?

David   Isn't that when you like everyone?

Jean   No, metrosexual's – that just means you moisturize and comb your hair.

David   No wait, pansexual, that's what I mean.

Jean   Oh Christ, don't it make you feel boring.

David   Well . . . It's been anything but boring, Jean.

We did some stuff, for round here. Didn't we? Just tell me we did, even if it's a lie.

Jean   . . . Course we did.

David   That, in spite of us being always at odds, with one another, each other's throats. Think what we might have done if we'd been friends.

Jean   Is that what we are now, then, have we made up?

David   Why could . . . why *couldn't* we ever just get along, me and you? Wasn't just the politics, was it, the . . . (*Sighs.*) I mean yes, not easy, ey? Working with someone so, alright, single-minded, stubborn, full of 'self-belief'?

Jean   No, of course it wasn't, but –

David   I was talking about.

Jean   Oh ha-ha-hah –

David *joins in with the mock-sarcastic laughing. They smile at one another . . .*

David   Anyway. At least you came back. (*Tapping the 'Independent' candidate on the flip chart.*) From enemy camp.

Jean   Yes, I'm . . . sorry about that . . . blip.

The TV continues to flicker. They watch.

Macaulay Culkin, that's it. Who I'm thinking of. With the – (*Imitates the emoji.*)

Right, I'll pour us another –

The phone rings. **Jean** *answers.*

Good morning, 'Death Row'?

OK. We'll start heading back.

David   Oh God, OK, ask. No, don't ask, just –

Jean (*to* **David**)   Do you want to know or not?

David   Alright, shit, no let's wait for the – no, fuck it, yes, ask, no don't.

Jean (*the phone*)   Hold on, David's developed some sort of election Tourette's.

David   Forget it, let's leave it.

Jean (*listens, on the phone*)   OK.

She puts the phone down, they both start to get ready to leave.

David   Either way it's shit, isn't it? Kicked out by 100 or just surviving by the same, hardly an endorsement.

Jean   Yeah well, that's the thing about politics, you come in through the front door, and they make you *leave* through the front as well.

David   Actually my first day in here, I think I came in through the back.

Jean (*opening the front door to look out*)   Is it raining? – No.

David   Go on then, tell me, did he tell you, what did he say?

Jean   Oh wind your neck in, he didn't tell me anything.

David   I know when you're lying, Jean Whittaker, look at me, I can tell.

He turns her round, holding her in front of him playfully.

Jean   What, no you can't, no one can, I'm like the *Daily Mail*, me.

David   Ey?

Jean   Unreadable.

David   I've been able to tell, all these years, I've just never said.

Jean   Oh is that so, all these years, really, well go on then, Uri Gagarin, read my mind.

David   Why Uri Gagarin?

Jean   Fella who bends spoons.

David   You daft twat, that's Uri Geller.

Jean   Same difference – go on then, what am I thinking now?

Elizabeth Lyons, *separated wife of* **David**, *walks in through the now open front door.* **Jean** *sees her first, over* **David**'s *shoulder, who doesn't.*

David . . . Now who could make my constituency agent, hard as nails, legend in her own town, who could make her face drop like that.

Nods, accepting the only possible answer. Without turning . . .

Hello Elizabeth.

He turns.

Elizabeth I'm sorry I should have . . .

I didn't mean to just turn up, out of the . . .

I'm interrupting something?

David Actually . . . well actually yes, my quarter of a century tenure as a Member of Parliament is about to come to an end, so –

Jean We don't know that, they're recounting, re-recounting, and actually / this one time –

Elizabeth Hello Jean.

Jean – hello Elizabeth. You look well. Sun must be shining in . . . I'm sorry I forget where you moved to.

Elizabeth Cambridge.

Jean Cambridge, blimey, how come you've been getting sun that little way down there, we've only had rain.

Elizabeth Not Cambridge, here. Cambridge, Massachusetts.

Jean There's *another* Cambridge University? In America?

Elizabeth Yeah, it's – Harvard. So . . .

Jean That's a good one, that one, isn't it. Well, world's top two universities, in two different Cambridges, who'd of thought? And that's where you live, is it?

Elizabeth It is, yes – well, over the river in Boston, yes.

Jean Boston like in Lincolnshire.

Elizabeth   No, this – again, this one is in Massachusetts. Jean. To save you time, I think there's basically two of everything. One here, one there.

Jean   So there's like, what, there's like two Newarks?

Elizabeth   There is actually, yes.

Jean   Two Yorks?

Elizabeth   Yes, that's – that's what *New* York is, isn't it.

Jean   Is there two Eccles?

Elizabeth   What?

Jean   I said is there two Eccles?

Elizabeth   Right, you're mocking me aren't you, good, I see nothing changes. Anyway, I wonder if I might speak to my hu- . . . my husband.

Jean   We've got to head to the Fesi Hall, they're calling it.

Elizabeth   David can probably speak for himself, though, can't he?

Jean   Actually . . . he – with the greatest of respect, Elizabeth, he –

Elizabeth   How is it that as soon as someone says 'with the greatest of respect' you know that they are about to tremendously disrespect you? Jean?

Jean   . . . We're still, technically, in the campaign, and I'm his election agent, and, until the result is called, this man's heart, and his soul, and particularly his mouth, actually, belongs to me, and not just his mouth, but his arse as well, because that's where he does most of his talking out of, so we don't want him to make any gaffes, repeat any mistakes. (*To* **David**, *pointedly.*) Right, David . . . we Do Not Want You . . . to Repeat the Same, Old, Mistake.

Elizabeth   I think I may have cracked your code, Jean.

David   Jean, it's OK. It's alright. Two minutes. I'll be fine.

Jean (*beat, then going to the door*)   Bye then, Elizabeth.

Elizabeth   Yeah see ya, Jean.

Jean *exits. Silence.*

David   I think I might lose my seat.

Elizabeth   . . . I think I might want you back.

Blackout.

Transition scenes 1–2

Music – as we reverse backwards . . .

These journeys can be a montage of movement full of 'local' moments on stage, interspliced with audio visual moments of 'national' events.

Regardless – in Act One, there should be a sense of reversing backwards . . .

David *votes in the May 2017 election, waving to the press.*

*Moving back to the campaign, with **Jean**, posing for photos with* **Constituents***, holding babies, all that.*

He makes a speech, on the stump.

David   Twenty-seven years, I've been proud to be your MP. Twenty-seven, that's longer than some marriages, older even than some countries and certainly, these days, some political parties. 'Time' can be good, time can mean stability, but it shouldn't mean old. It shouldn't mean stuck. So I promise – in these times that can feel scarier, and more uncertain than ever – I want to look forward, not back. I don't want to repeat, I want to renew. And I relish the opportunity to throw my hat in the ring once more. To ask you to come *with* me, again, another time . . .

. . . thank you.

Backwards through –

Theresa May getting into power, Cameron resigning – the Referendum – Jeremy Corbyn replacing Ed Miliband – marches against austerity – riots in the street – Ed Miliband replacing Gordon Brown . . .

Scene Two

January, 2011. Midday.

The remnants of some half-arsed Christmas decorations, limply scattered about.

Jean *comes in the front door (no locks or security), holding Aldi shopping bags, flicking the lights on.*

Jean   Oh, shit.

She checks the time and dumps her bags. Notices a Dancing Snowman doll on the desk. She claps. It begins to dance, singing a few lines of Frosty the Snowman.

She unpacks her bags full of scones, jam, various spray cans, and begins taking down decorations.

David *enters quickly, out of the cold.*

David   So far so good, I think . . . (*Seeing the decorations.*) Oh, Jesus.

Jean   I know, it's fine.

David   What's all this still doing up?

Jean   Well, we weren't meant to be here today, were we? And no one's been back in since before Christmas, have they? So –

David   This is bad.

Jean   I know, it's the 8th, you're meant to have it all down by the 6th, it's bad luck.

David   That's not what I meant, Jean, I meant it looks bad for our very, very important guest. We look like amateurs. What's that smell?

Jean   The dead tree – it's alright, I've got air freshener, I'm on it. Apple and cinnamon, nice and wintery.

She sprays some into the air from her bag.

Margot Midler *enters. She's early 40s here, the Deputy Council Leader.*

Margot   I got your message. He left the site just after me, he's probably about five minutes behind.

Jean   Margot, I'm sorry, I know you're the great and wonderful Deputy Leader of the council now, but please, pretty please can you help unpack these bits and bobs, we're on the clock. It's the best I could find at short notice. I went for traditional cream tea, I thought he might find it, you know – quaint.

Margot   And it's really too cold at the Fesi Hall?

Jean   Boiler's packed in. We'll be fine, nice and cosy, more intimate.

David   Of all the days for Len to go AWOL, Jean?

Margot   What, I'm not good enough for you? I *can* do this, you know –

David   I know, I know, but Deputy Leader isn't Leader, is it. It's not as . . . Jean? Come on, he's your husband.

Jean   Don't ask me. Professional – personal; personal – professional.

Margot *(taking out a variety of spray tins)*   God, look at these. Used to be a Morrisons here, and before that a Tesco. That's a better indicator than GDP, ey David? From Tescos to Aldi in three short years.

David   Well, that's why we need this contract, isn't it, which is why the next – *(Watch.)* half hour needs to go / well, doesn't it?

Margot   What's that smell?

Jean   Dead Christmas tree, spray that. Apple and cinnamon. No, wait, that's David's deodorant, Christ, 'no frills', everything looks the same. Here.

Margot sprays.

David   He's a multi-millionaire, Jean, I'm not sure about scones from Aldi. What if we actually sent out for, like a Chinese, a gesture of, like –

Jean   *He's* Chinese, you can't feed Chinese to a Chinese person.

Margot   Yeah, isn't that, like, cannibalism?

David   What – it – Chinese food isn't made up 'of' Chinese people, is it!

Jean   Margot, can you fetch me some plates, sorry, I know, just all hands to the pump, chop chop!

She claps – the Dancing Snowman begins again.

They look at it. **Margot** *exits into the kitchenette.* **Jean** *shoves it in a drawer as they continue.*

Jean   We need to work out our answer on skills, that's what he'll ask about.

David   Did she say anything? Margot? About . . .?

Jean   No, I didn't ask. You were on the tour of the site with her; *you* ask.

David   She shouldn't even be here, it should be the Council Leader.

Jean   I'm not calling him, David, how many times? Personal – professional, he's not my husband as at work, is he? Wherever he is, that's where he is. Margot knows her stuff.

David   Then why is she resigning her post? I have it on good authority –

Jean   Oh rubbish, why would she just quit?

David   Why do you think? She's wants to *stand,* in 2015. I've got my own eyes and ears on the CLP, Jean, I think someone in the Cabinet is trying for a coup, to deselect me, it could be her –

Jean   Ohmygod, you always think – you're like that kid in *The Sixth Sense*, except you see deselection everywhere, all the time. She's not –

Margot *re-enters from the back with some plates.*

Margot   Best I could do. Had to wash them up.

Jean *squirts some more cream onto some jam and scones.*

Jean   There. See? English cream tea, all for less than a tenner.

David   Oh, arse, my presentation. The power point – all the gear's at the . . . (*A breath.*) It's fine, simple is better. Words.

Jean (*gasping with excitement*)   Wait, I know! It's still here, isn't it? (*Running out into the back – off.*) Did we throw it out?

David   No, *don't*, I know what you're thinkin- . . . Oh fuck a duck.

Margot   Car's pulled up.

David   Jean, the car's pulled up!

Jean *enters with her flipchart on a rickety old stand.*

Jean   Look! Good as new! My board, oh how I've missed my board.

David   I'm still bored of your board; I'm still –

Jean (*flipping through some old pages*)   Oh the brainstorming we did on this over the years, only way to properly think. Campaign messages, policy work. Not had a single good idea since you made us go all digital.

David   Well, that we can agree on.

Margot   I'll fetch him in. Do you trust me with that, or should I just stick to pot-washing? (*She opens the front door, doing a 'Chinese greeting', hands together.*) Ni Hao!

David   God, I wish she wouldn't do that, borderline racist.

Jean   I could try some of the lingo – it's been a while, but –

David   No, no, please.

Jean   Alright, come on let me look at you. (*With* **David**, *fussing.*) Remember, calm, cool, we're not desperate, we're just the right choice, plain and simple –

David   Funnily enough, I remember handling complex and important negotiations when I was the Secretary of State for Trade and Industry, Jean.

Jean   Well, not being funny but that was a long time ago.

David   Well, they say multimillion pound corporate trade deals are like riding a bike, don't they. You always look a bit of a twat doing them.

Jean   Alright, just calm, breathe, chill . . .

Margot *leads in* **Mr. Shen** – *a Chinese investor.*

Margot   – Yeah, they're deliberately not very grand, constituency offices, meant to be just like any other shop on the high street. You've met Mr. Lyons, this morning.

Shen   Thank you for receiving me. I hear there was a problem at the –?

David   Hello again, yes the Festival Hall, our leisure centre, we had a whole thing planned, with – banners, and things, but this cold weather, it's knocked out the –

Shen   I assumed England was always this cold – or is that just the movies?

Gentle laughter.

David   Yes, and we're always the baddies.

Shen   I don't know, I think we might soon be catching you up there.

Jean   Jean Whittaker. I'm the office manager, and David's, um, agent, and a lot of things, how do you do.

Shen   Hello. (*Sniffs, uncertainly.*) That smell, is that – lunch?

Jean   Uh, no, that's just –

Margot   Here, let me take your coat?

As **Margot** *turns him towards the coat stand,* **Jean** *sprays her air freshener.*

Except . . . it's the squirty cream, and a plume of white foam ejects into the air, landing on the bag that **Shen** *carried in with him and placed on the table.*

David *and* **Jean** *and* **Margot** *stare in silent panic at one another as* **Margot** *tries to lead* **Shen** *around the office without him seeing, looking at photos on the wall.*

Margot   And so these are, uh, some photos over – what is it now David, twenty-one years he has been the MP here, so . . .

Shen   This is the quarry when it was open?

Jean *follows behind her with a cloth, wiping the floor.*

David   Yes, proud industrial heritage, this town.

She leads him towards into the back kitchenette so he's momentarily out of the office.

Jean   It's fine, he didn't notice.

She puts the squirty cream down, picks up the air freshener and sprays as **David** *frantically wipes the bag clean with the cloth.*

David   Jesus, I'm sweating.

He picks up the deodorant for under his shirt, she picks up the squirty cream for the scones.

Jean   Calm down, just give him one of these, mm, yum.

She sprays cream onto her final scone – only it's not cream, it's deodorant.

Jean   Wait!

Too late – he sprays the squirty cream under his shirt.

They stare at one another, frozen, as **Shen** *comes back in.*

Shen   A nice little office you have, Mr. Lyons.

David (*lowering his arm, as gently as possible*)   David, please.

Jean   Cream and jam scone, Mr. Shen? English delicacy?

Shen   . . . Thank you. The rest of my group are already at the football match?

David   Oh, yes, you're right, we should get cracking.

He claps his hands together to 'mean business'. From the drawer, the Dancing Snowman begins its song, as everyone slowly sits, pretending they can't hear it, **David** *trying not to squelch his creamy armpit.*

David   We really just thought, in addition to touring our proposed site for your plant at the old quarry, it would be good to have a private chat, to put our case to you properly. Prove we're the – the erm . . . the *cream* of the crop, ahah. Erm –

Shen   We have your proposed outline, it's all there in black and white –

David   No, I know, I know, but. We know you have offers from Zeebrugge, and Gdansk. But I suppose I wanted to communicate personally, how . . . how hungry, we are, for this. Our location is unparalleled, right?

Margot   Smack bang between the M1 and the A1 –

David   Yep, the, the main arteries that run through Britain. We have . . . there is a large potential workforce, sat there, waiting, raring to go –

Shen   But they are – untrained, in these sorts of skills, no? And currently unemployed? Many thousands . . .?

David   We . . . areas like this, the economic down- . . . we're particularly vulnerable, with so many jobs in the public

sector, to cuts from this new government, it's the same cycle
we went through, areas like this, under the *last* Tory
governments, time and time again, and –

Shen   Since the quarry closed, and before that the coal
mines – the main source of employment has been these new
government centres, am I right?

Jean   The Data Centre, yes. It's a – *was,* a records bureau;
the government digitized all public records, and so it acts,
acted as like a central call centre too.

Shen   Call centre for what?

Jean   To – to transfer calls. Between government
departments. All the hotlines were amalgamated into one
central one, here. David fought hard, very hard –

Shen   So people phone this new hotline, that the
government pays for, to send them to the same department,
where the phone lines were cut?

David   . . . It – when the quarry . . . there's been limestone
mining, in this area, for centuries but, as the work
disappeared to . . . (*Gesturing, ironically.*), well other
countries, the effects of globalization, all that, we needed
something to be built 'on top', of the holes. Jobs that would
lead to spending and lead to growth and then to jobs that
could sustain themselves, and –

Shen   So, before, there was government money pouring
into these quarries, and mines, across the land, digging for
things you no longer needed. Your answer was to fill in those
holes, and build on top these 'centres'. Which you didn't
really need. And . . . now they're closing too? Is that not
work for work's sake?

David *takes a beat. Calm, now. A flash, perhaps, of the politician
of old.*

David   Mr. Shen. We *can* make things, here, we can build
your trains, it's in our DNA, with just a bit of training –

Shen   Of course. Once the 'workshop of the world', this country, of course.

David   Yes, in fact, Arkwright's mill, the first ever factory, Spinning Jenny, just down the road, what fifteen, twenty minutes drive from here?

Margot   About that. I could check. (*On her phone.*)

David   You don't need to check, just –

Shen   Really? The first factory?

David   Yep, birthed the industrial revolution. Without which, no trains, no . . . Apple, no Google, no nothing.

Margot   Yeah, twenty-three minutes it says, by car. Or you could cycle in one hour thirty-one, it says. (*Showing him her Google maps.*)

David   And, look, I negotiated a government guarantee of capital –

Margot   Oh wait, no, shit, that's from my house –

David   – Yes, thank you, Margot; our inclusion into their 500 million pound government guarantee of shared capital investment which should make coming *here* . . . a little more palatable.

Shen   Tempting us with 'gifts', hmm? I read that you personally got – what's the phrase, a lot of 'stick', for that. Working with the enemy party.

David   I'm a pragmatist, Mr. Shen.

Shen   A pragmatist over an idealist?

David   No point in having ideals if you have no means by which to deliver them. Ideals don't put bread on the table. This is what I do, Mr. Shen; I get things done.

Shen   Well. Our decision will be transparent, and most important, quick.

Margot   We should get you to the Forest game.

Shen (*standing*)   Yes, 'Nottingham Forest'. Where Robin Hood used to live, right? 'Robbing from the rich to give to the poor.' The first real socialist.

David   Aha, yes, a proud Nottinghamshire lad.

Shen   Your party? You no longer sing the *Red Flag*, is that right? 'We'll keep it flying here'. You no longer sing this, it no longer flies?

David   It's still sung, in – some quarters.

Shen   We still fly ours, of course, haha. Although we too found our 'third way' – was that what he called it? We are now in our 'Third Plenum'. The old values, but with . . . (*Gesturing* **David**.) 'economic pragmatism'. You would describe yourself as – Democratic Socialists, I think, here?

David   Uh, Jean would, I'm more a . . . Social Democrat.

Margot   I've never thought to define myself anything; what's the difference?

David   Well, crudely, she's got more socialist in hers and I've got more democrat in mine, but it's all cheese on the same board.

Jean (*as a private dig*)   Although I think of you more as a Social Corporatist sometimes, David.

David   Do you, Jean?

Margot   Is that another one?

Shen   This new Scottish government? They are on the Left?

David   Yes, but they have – I suppose they're a popular nationalist movement, with Social Democratic tendencies –

Jean   *Democratic* Socialist –

David   Democratic Socialist tendencies. But they're a nationalist party too.

Margot   Oh well, I like them, that's me then, I'm a *National* Socialist.

David/Jean   No.

David   No, you're not, Margot, not a National Socialist.

Margot   Am I not?

David/Jean   No.

Margot   Oh.

Shen   Well. Thank you for clearing all that up. And for your hospitality.

David   Bye then, take care.

Shen *leaves, lead by* **Margot**. *A moment.*

David (*to* **Jean**, *questioningly*)   Well that . . . went . . . OK?

Jean (*beat . . . pacing . . . shaking her head*).   He'll not bring it here.

David   What, why?

Jean   Dunno, sixth sense, women's intuition, I dunno just something.

David   I think that . . . Jean, could you not at least like *pretend* that I did an alright job, maybe once? / I actually think we have a real shot at –

Jean   You did, I'm just saying, it was – it feels rigged against us from the off. You heard him, the 'tempting with gifts' thing. I dunno, maybe we should have been less desperate, a bit of integrity.

David   Integr- . . . right.

Jean   Not you, *us*, it, everyone, you're / yet again misinterpreting what I'm–

David   No I get it, thank you very much.

David *drops a file down onto his desk. The slap starts the Snowman up again in the drawer.*

David   Oh for –!

He begins opening drawer after drawer, trying to find it, but he can't.

David   Where is it?!

Jean *nonchalantly opens the drawer nearest to her and holds up the Snowman.*

David   Right.

He takes it and exits at speed out of the back. **Jean**'s *Blackberry rings, she answers.*

Jean   Where've *you* been? You-know-who is going spare, he thought you'd be here.

Margot (*coming back in through the front*)   Where's David?

Jean   Killing a snowman. 'In cold blood.' (*On the phone.*) Alright, I'll see you at home, talk then. Bye. (*Hangs up.*)

David (*re-entering*)   That's the last we'll see of him.

Margot   You don't think he's going to pick us?

David   The snowman, not Mr. Shen. Why is everyone so negative on –

Margot   Is there no other strings you can pull?

David   If you recall, Margot, Labour got kicked out of office last year, so I'm –

Margot   What about other folk, influential people, used to boast about your 'direct line' to Tony Blair, couldn't he put a word in?

David   Nope, that's a while back now, and anyway, all the direct lines were amalgamated into one centralised call centre, so –

Margot   Is that meant to be funny?

Jean's *Blackberry rings. She looks at the caller I.D.*

Jean   Well, get to the foot of my stairs.

(*Answers.*) Whoever this is, we're calling the police for stealing Cheryl's phone, no way would she be working on a Saturday. There's all them repeats to watch of – I can't think of anything funny.

Margot   *All Creatures Great and Small.*

Jean   Why's that funny?

Margot   Dunno.

Jean (*on the phone*)   No, why? Cheryl, it's only a journalist. Just get back to your crossword or whatever; we'll speak Monday. (*Hangs up.*)

David   What?

Jean   Nothing, just in a flap about that *Telegraph* woman, she's still chasing, another round of expenses stories.

David   I haven't claimed for anything that I – have I? Squeaky clean. Lemme speak to her.

Jean   No, just ignore her. Don't let your ego get the better of you.

David   My ego?

Jean   You know what I mean.

David   No, I don't know want you mean and I'd like you to clarify please.

Jean (*a moment. Then, overly professional*)   Forgive me, Mr. Lyons, I simply meant that you have taken a lot of knocks of late and some woman from the *Telegraph* offering to puff up your national profile again could make you say something you don't mean, simply by appealing to your vanity which, permit me, is the size of the Thames estuary. Mr. Lyons, master, sir.

David Thanks for your incomparable political expertise as ever, Jean.

Jean Welcome.

David That Open University course just keeps paying for itself doesn't it.

Jean *had been making to go, opening the front door. This makes her stops . . .*

David . . . Look, I –

Jean (*launching back*) Do you know what – he's right, that fella, he could see this place and all that's been 'achieved' for what it was. All looks good on the outside but it only takes one little tremor to bring the whole thing down.

David Tremor? / Do you mean the worldwide financial collapse?

Jean – Showing how utterly empty it all was on the inside, how utterly –

David Empty, right, this from the person whose job it is to / champion –

Jean Job? My job / is to help the people of this town –

David How come you *never,* you never ever mention the long list of – (*Counting on his fingers.*) I don't know, every school here – refurbished, rebuilt! The bloody – the two bloody city centres, regenerated! Three hospitals, /almost entirely rebuilt.

Jean Yeah, spending, good, fine, but not the actual difficult work of digging deep down, into the underlying factors woven into the rotten fabric of this unfair, fucking country.

David No, you're right, I'm sorry, I'll put that on my to-do list, shall I?

(*At her flipchart, writing 'To do'.*) 'Morning, walk the dog, afternoon, single-handedly uproot the systematic inequalities and injustices woven into British society.'

Jean   OK fine, do it your way, your third way, just 'accepting' the long and inevitable decline round here, finding a way just to make it 'tolerable' instead. A dead Christmas tree wrapped up in shitty tinsel and a tatty fucking star.

David   Oh yes, I know I've never been enough, Jean, I was never going to live up to my predecessor, the all-seeing, all-knowing, can't do no wrong late husband who got all the way up the ladder to, remind me, which *junior* post in the *shadow* cabinet?

Jean (*beat. Turns to go*)   Fuck it, don't know why I stay here.

David   No, well I don't think you ever really *were* here, were you, not really.

Jean *makes to turn back to him, upset, but stops and leaves, slamming the door. A beat.* **Margot** *sits, quietly.*

David   Never once – never *once*, believed in anything that I . . .

He kicks a something over. Silence.

Margot   Dunno how you haven't *killed* each other, you two. All these . . .

David   Sorry. I know you're . . . you're worried about your family. Jobs. I'm . . .

Margot   Is she right? They won't pick us?

David (*beat. Shrugs*)   Flip a coin . . .

Margot   A coin? So what, just – luck, and fate, then? Isn't that what 'politics' is meant to prevent? MPs, or councillors, or whoever, not just leaving things to chance, but to try to control . . . to *shape* things. Our own –

David   OK, well, yes / that's –

She's on her feet now, pacing, getting more worked up . . .

Margot   I mean I've tried. Over the road, God knows, you don't feel like you're achieving much, most of the time, hardly any of the time, and all my friends, ha! 'Local government, why the hell do you . . .?' and I *didn't* want to, at first, can't even remember why I did, but I did, and I thought that, you know, you'd pull a lever, push a button, and Make A Difference –

David   Alright, I know, OK –

Margot   But you push it, you pull it, nothing happens! Just . . . forces, way beyond your . . . And yet here's you, get to hop off to Westminster, half the week, swanning around as the Big –

David   OK, I know / this is – upsetting . . . Margot . . .

Margot   While down there they slash and they cut us up here, our budget halved then halved again, soon all we'll be, all we'll do is just . . . cut grass. Now and again. That's what local government will be, and that's *not* what I . . .

David   . . . Alright, so what would you do? If you . . . just hypothetically, of course, Margot. But what would you do, if you were the MP? Here?

Margot   . . . Why, what's the point? There is no 'here' anymore . . .

She exits the office. Silence.

David *rips off the flipchart sheet he'd scribbled on, absent-mindedly turning the pages. A lot of his and Jean's 'thinking' over the years, 'messaging' . . .*

. . . until he sees one. One he doesn't recognise. Looks like **Jean**'s *handwriting from before. He reads it aloud, tragi-comically at first any then . . . less so . . .*

David   'David – twat.' – No surprise there, then.
  'Little me – without future . . .
  Any view? Never.
  Could I stand? . . . (*Beat.*)
  Under you. Can't, why?
  This. Admit. Too scared.
  You are. Why?'

David, *confused . . . sitting back, trying to make sense of it. He grows in anger, clenching his fists . . . trying to calm . . .*

He goes to his desk and accesses his phone message on speaker — 'For new messages, press 1. For saved messages, press 2.' *— He presses 2, and paces, pouring himself a drink.*

Voice (*voice recording*)   'Uh, David, it's Sahill at the Council . . . so look, just between us, Margot Midler wants to leave her post as Deputy and . . . well, we're interested in getting Jean Whittaker in. I know you rely on her, but we need someone with local standing for that Ward and, you know, it could be good for her too, I think, a springboard for a . . . whatever, so yeh. It's a courtesy call. Tell me what you think.'

David *hangs up. Beat. He re-dials.*

David   Sahill. David Lyons. Sorry to call on a Saturday, but you called me, yer bastard. Anyway, Jean Whittaker . . .

. . . uh, look. I would say – I would say '*no*'. Actually. I don't think you should take her on. She's . . . her heart's in the right place. But . . . I would personally look elsewhere.

Lights begin to fade.

Transition scenes 2–3

Backwards we go –

The Conservative Lib-Dem coalition is formed – Gordon Brown leaves Downing Street with his family – Labour having been kicked out after thirteen years.

Locally, **David** *opens an Academy school – cuts the ribbon on the new Data Centre – makes a speech on the local 2005 campaign trail –*

David   More jobs, more homes, more opportunities – we have managed to end the Tory boom and bust. It is with great pleasure, and gratitude, that I am returned as your MP, for a fourth election running!

The 2005 election Labour victory: minimal turnout, reduced majority – the 7/7 bombings – War in Iraq – people marching on the street to prevent the war – the attacks of 9/11.

Scene Three

June, 2001. Afternoon.

Election campaign detritus around the place. Some promotional material for the new data centre. Maps of the different Wards and the flip chart with rolling turnout figures for different areas.

Jean *is leaning against her desk, having a brief moment.*

Some noise, approaching the front door. She gets herself together as **David** *enters – waving bye to some* **Party Activists** *outside. A jubilant mood.*

David   Yep, brilliant! Thank you, keep at it, I'll see you later.

Once the door is closed he does a little mock-dance towards her.

Ra-tah-rah-, a-rat-tat-tah, well! I don't mean to tempt fate or anything, but this is the closest I've felt to being a rock star. Do you think it's too hubristic to say I don't think the Conservatives, the self-appointed natural party of government, are ever going to get back in again?

Jean   Yes, I do think that's hubristic. (*Scribbling on her flipchart and the wall of different local wards.*) Right, latest numbers from my Presiding Officer in Carsic, that's our second highest Labour voting ward, turnout out down 4 per cent on '97, but not by the margins its up in Tory wards, so we're still on track.

Fourth victory in a row for you here, David, well done.

David   Well done *you*, thank you, good – really good campaign.

Jean   Oh well, like you say, a lemon could get in here if it was Labour, so.

David   Oy stop being down on yourself, mard arse, / doesn't suit you.

Jean   I'm not – oy, you're the mardy one.

David I'm the *lucky* one, having the agent with the most efficient GOTV machine in the country, renowned.

Jean Oh shut up, it's just common sense.

David So have I finally converted you to the ways of winning, Jean Whittaker, a centrist government in power rather than purist left opposition?

Jean . . . I can reluctantly see some of the benefits, yes.

David I promise we'll do something with it. Those spending ceilings were a first term commitment only. It's not just winning for winning's sake. We can change things, we can – build.

Margot – *currently a relatively junior council worker* – *enters with plastic bags.*

Margot Alright. Just dropping off these leftover leaflets, I finished up at Nuncargate. And I filled in the forms, asking the questions this time – so sorry I forgot, idiot. 'How did you vote last time', 'who you voting for this time' –

Jean Thanks Margot, know it's a pain but it's how we keep track of which way we're swinging – (*grabbing some new flyers*), right it's 4 o'clock so we need you to move onto the third leaflets now.

Margot Third leaflets? I thought I was / done?

Jean Three leaflets as part our GOTV strategy, get out the vote, this is our 'There's Still Time' one for the school run home, and end of shifts – thank you.

Margot No worries. All sounds good though, right? Home and dry?

David It does, Margot, yeah.

Margot All those new jobs at the centre, that'll be why. My uncle Mark, he just got a position as a, a, erm, an inputting –

David A data inputter.

Margot   An inputter, exactly. Fifteen years he worked in that quarry, my Aunt Mary couldn't get dust out his clothes, and now he's a 'data inputter'. I didn't think he knew what digital was.

Jean   You should see my new washer-dryer, Margot, that's digital. It's got a timer, you can set it. In fact I've got a wash that'll just be going on now.

Margot   And you're not even there?

Jean   And I'm not even there, I know! I use mine as an alarm, don't I, David? I set it to go off in the morning. Nothing wakes you up like a spin cycle.

David   Why don't you come here just before the count if you'll like, little BBQ for the members – thanking everyone who helped out.

Margot   Are you sure? Oh, well, thank you, that's –

Jean   Come on, here's a list of phone numbers, volunteer drivers the party's insured to give elderly and disabled a lift to the polling station – only Labour voters though, obviously!

Margot   Oh, OK. Eek! Exciting, this proper politics stuff, ey? Like being in a film.

She leaves through the front door.

Jean   Well remind me never to go to the pictures with her.

David   Are your lads coming to the count tonight, celebrate?

Jean   Oh, don't, you should take this as a compliment, but they're bored of you winning. Anyway two have school tomorrow.

David   Len will be joining later too –

Jean   Awh Jesus, that gobshite. What, coming to take credit for nothing?

David   He's the CLP Secretary, we need to be joined up, don't wanna get complacent. And after all. (*Begins a kind of cheeky 'jig' towards her, semi-singing.*) Dare I say it . . . as a future big beast in the party . . . in the Brand New Cabinet . . . I think there might just . . . be cameras there this time, ra-tat-tah-tah . . .

Jean (*can't not laugh*)   You daft plonker.

(*Regains herself.*) And don't be so bloody arrogant.

David   Awh, I was trying to be cute.

Jean   Oh, well, 'Jean to mission control, abort, abort'. God, you really can't dance, can you?

David   Oh is that what you think? Well, if you must know –

Jean   So come on then (*At her flip chart.*), TV sensation of the future, what do you want to talk about with the eyes of the world, watching?

David   New investment in the town, obviously, specifically the data centre, specifically plans to extend the tram here from the city, specifically –

Jean   Unapproved by the council –

David   As is everything until I twist their arm, ad infinitum, and –

Jean   Say something about the new school.

David   Hark who's changed her tune on the new school.

Jean   I haven't, I stand by the old school – that was a good school, and still reckon there's no place for profit in education / that's all I'm saying –

David   It's not profit, it's just *private* money, getting fat cats to pay back into society, win win.

Jean   I went to that old school, Mum was a dinner lady at that school, it was a good school –

David There were holes in the roof of that school – and, oy, I – (*Losing his humour now, momentarily.*) I also went to that school, briefly, remember, you seem to . . . uggh, honestly, every opportunity to make me feel like I'm not a –

Jean Oh, go fly a kite, you. Honestly, *you* take every opportunity to / willfully misinterpret everything I've said, it's your bloody insecurities –

David Alright, AL-RIGHT! Jesus, can there not just be one occasion where we don't end up bloody well . . . (*Deep breath.*) and just effing *celebrate* . . .

. . . I got you something.

He pulls down a small screen on the wall, opens up a laptop on his desk, presses a key and voila. A power point projection.

Jean What is it?

David Ta-da. (*Kicking her rickety old flip chart.*) I know how you like to, you know, visualize a problem, work it out. Twentieth century thinking but via twenty-first century means.

Jean Is this is gift for me or for you, I'm not gonna be able to work that.

David 'Thank you, David, that's very kind of you.'

Jean Thank you, David, that's very kind of you, but I didn't ask for it.

David I think you've just described a sodding *present*. Jean. Look –

(*Demonstrates.*) Here's the viability report on the tram line extension. And, look, here's my idea for a slogan. (*A logo of the word 'trams'.*) See?

Jean It just says 'trams'. Wow, that's inspiring.

David What do trams do? They go forwards *and* back. And what is 'trams' backwards? . . . '*Smart*'. Yeah? It's a palindrome. A palindrome and a metaphor.

Jean   No it's not. It's not a palindrome, that's when it's the same word one way as it is the other, like, er, erm, 'level'. Or . . . 'Oxo'.

David   Oh yeah, alright, fine it's not a palindrome, but it's still a metaphor. What works going into the city, works travelling out, into the towns as well. Bringing opportunities, see?

Jean   It's a mirror. One of those mirror poems. 'Am I clever? Clever, I am'.

David   Well, now you just sound like Yoda.

The phone rings. **David** *answers.*

David   Hello . . . Cheryl, hi . . . what's the . . . (*Beat. He sits slowly.*)

Oh. Erm. OK. I'll try her, erm . . . her cell. Mobile, I mean. Thank you.

He puts phone down. A beat. Speaking quite carefully, trying to stay calm?

Elizabeth. She wasn't on the plane.

Jean   Elizabeth? She was . . . ? She's – coming back? Tonight? You two are –?

David   Just . . . for tonight. A show of unity. You know. 'On the tele.' But then . . . we were . . . I thought we were . . . going to 'see'. We were going to . . . 'talk'.

Jean   You never said? Why didn't you say?

Well that's . . . that's good news; good for you, yeah, you should –

David   Cheryl waited. At – arrivals. Heathrow. But she wasn't on the plane.

Beat. **David** *picks up the phone. And dials.*

A knock at the door, a **Delivery Man** *enters with a bouquet of red roses.*

Delivery   Flowers? For –

Jean (*jumping up*)   Yeah – it – I'll sign, for . . .

David (*on the phone*)   Hi. Me. Call me back. Although given this rang with an international dial tone . . . I'm guessing I should make alternative plans for tonight. Erm . . . I can't think of anything else to say but I don't appear to be hanging up . . .

(*After a beat, he hangs up. Beat.*) Who are they from?

Jean   Dunno, flowers, for you, I think – I dunno, it doesn't say.

David   . . . From her? Why would she send me flowers? What do they mean?

Jean   I've no idea, I've never understood her, sorry. I'll put them in some –

Jean *exits.* **David** *sits, limply.*

Jean (*off*)   Bollocks, I smashed that vase the other week, erm – oh, hold on.

Jean *comes back, with a Wellington boot.*

Jean   Here. What? I ran some water into it; not going to leak is it, that's the whole point of a wellie.

She sets the boot down and arranges the flowers into it. They stare at it.

David   Roses. What roses mean, remember. 'The words you cannot say.'

It's a message.

Fade around them, as lights linger on the bright red roses . . .

Transition scenes 3–4

Moving backwards, still . . . quicker now . . .

New Labour's first term – Tony Blair entering Downing Street – the 1997 election – the 'New Labour' rebrand – the 1995 conference and the abolition of Clause IV.

Scene Four

July, 1994. Evening.

A brass band is warming up outside.

Elizabeth *stands facing* **David** *either side of the fax machine.*
David *is holding a sheet of paper, delaying the sending of it. They're staring at each other, when . . .*

. . . **Jean** *comes in through the front door.*

Jean (*to those outside*)   Three minutes! (*Inside.*) David, come on! Oh. Elizabeth. You made it.

Elizabeth   Yes, I – it . . . felt important.

Jean   The ceremony?

Elizabeth   The what?

Jean   For the quarry closing?

Elizabeth   . . . Oh, yes –

Jean (*seeing the sheet*)   Heavens to betsy, you haven't sent it yet?!

David   I am doing, we are doing, we've – decided.

Jean   'We'?

David   I'm pressing send now, I just needed a moment to . . .

Jean   They're ready to go, I want you to lead the procession.

David   Lead? No, they don't want me leading, / can't I just –

Jean   It'll help their like, perception, of you. Oy, you asked for me help with this kind of thing, well this is my help, this is what it looks like – get your arse outside.

On the TV, the 1994 Labour leadership election. Senior party figures, being interviewed in studios.

David   There they all are, look. My 'peers', a million miles away.

Jean   Yeah well, what's happening here is more important than a leadership election. Fax your nomination in and come on.

She heads upstairs. **Elizabeth** *hisses quietly at* **David***, as –*

Elizabeth   David, this is serious. If we're . . . –

– they're interrupted, by **Len Prior***, the Council Leader, entering through the front office door. He's London born, nominally middle-class, with a slightly affected working-class tone . . .*

Len   Tick tock, the procession is about to 'process'. Like the Chartists and Jarrow marchers before them.

David   Elizabeth, this is Len, leader of the council and also the Secretary for the local party. Len, this is my wife –

Len   Ah hello, *Mrs.* Lyons. The Lion-ness! Haha. My hours in front of David Attenborough tell me, I *think*, that it is the female lion who does all the hunting – is that right, David? It would explain the boots.

Elizabeth (*at her Wellingtons – the ones we'll see again in 2001*) Oh, yes, no one else is wearing – is it too much?

Len   Don't mind me, I shouldn't even really be in here. Council, Party; Party, Council – 'delineation'. I'm just looking for Jean. She's giving me the horn.

Elizabeth   She's what?

Len   To play, in the band.

Jean *comes back down the stairs holding an instrument case.*

Jean   Here, sorry, so much crap up there, must start chucking stuff away.

Len   Thanking you. (*Removes from the case, does some toots.*) Terry won't mind?

Jean   Course not, it'll cheer him up? David, seriously, we have to go. I'll do it –

David (*typing in the phone number at speed*)   No no, it's OK, I've got it.

Jean   He's sulking because we made him opt for John, not Tony.

David   Not sulking, I don't 'sulk', Jean, I have ideological differences –

Elizabeth   *Personal* differences, these are our friends.

Len   Oof, friends with 'The Blairs', ey?

David   Not *friends* just – Elizabeth studied law at the same college as Cherie.

Len   Criminal?

Elizabeth   To be friends with the Blairs? Not the last time I checked.

Len   Criminal law –

Elizabeth   Yes I know what you – . . . And no, corporate. And we weren't the same year. Obviously. She's much –

Len   Corporate lawyers in the Labour party?! I recall the heady days when our membership was apprentices and craftsmen. Labourers and –

Elizabeth   Corporations are businesses, businesses create jobs, I would've thought that's exactly what you needed, round here, is it not?

Len   Must put personal feelings aside in politics, our constituency labour party passed a motion favouring Prescott, and it's right their view is respected.

Elizabeth   Yes, but it's not their name on the voting ballot is it, it's David's, it only reflects on him. Him *and* me.

Jean (*at her wellies*)   Going hiking, Elizabeth?

Elizabeth   See, I knew – . . . I wasn't sure what to expect, I thought a 'quarry', you know, sludge and stuff.

Jean   You don't want to ruin those anyway, look spotless.

Elizabeth   I got them for a festival.

Len   Festival! Which one, Glastonbury? Reading?

Elizabeth   Do you know Hay-on-Wye?

Len   Can't say I do.

Elizabeth   I had a book talk there. Just a little legal book I wrote, only small.

Jean   Ooh, I love those legal thrillers. Like John Grisham? What's it called?

Elizabeth   'Putting the Share in Shareholdings – Progressive Opportunities in Commerce and Trade.'

Jean (*beat*)   I like that *Pelican Brief* one, have you read that?

Len (*to* **Elizabeth**)   My flugelhorn's bent out of shape, thought about getting a new one. But – got to be frugal with me flugal. Haha. Want a go?

Elizabeth   Oh – no, thank you.

Len   Go on, give it a puff. Oop, as the bishop said to the – something.

Elizabeth   Oh, er, do you have a . . .

She tries to discreetly wipe the mouthpiece with her sleeve as he thrusts it towards her mouth, before giving the horn a little ineffective blow.

Len   Ah, see? Takes practice, that's all. You know I was once entered into the regionals. I got a certificate.

Elizabeth   Talk about blowing your own horn.

Len   Well, I was only saying.

Elizabeth   No, I know, it – I was – right anyway I'm taking these off. (*Sits.*)

Len   Onwards Christian soldiers. (*He leaves through the front door.*)

Jean   Here, I'll give you a hand –

She grabs **Elizabeth***'s feet and yanks the boots off, hard,* **Elizabeth** *having to hold on.*

Jean   There, I'll put them out the way for you – David SEND THE FUCKING FORM NOW!

David   I AM!

Jean *goes upstairs.* **Elizabeth** *removing some high heels out of her bag.*

Elizabeth   You could have chipped in a bit there, couldn't you? How come no one ever knows when I'm joking up here, it's like there's a humour deficiency or something, it – I can't – like a different language.

Outside, the brass band strikes up. The Red Flag.

Elizabeth   Oh you – are – kidding. Is there going to be local press, cameras?

David   Well I hope so, yes –

Elizabeth   The matt- . . . can't you hear that? What is it, oh I like this one, is it *Too Shy* by Kajagoogoo – oh no wait, my mistake, it's the *Red fucking Flag!*

David   I know, you think I don't know? But round here it's a 'process', small steps, I can't / rattle every cage in one go.

Elizabeth   You don't see how you, *us*, being seen out there, with that playing, is directly contradicting what is happening down there (*The TV.*), with our lot? How –

Jean (*returning*)   Right, that's it, if I have to throw you out I will, come on.

Beat. **Elizabeth** *exits.* **Jean** *glares at* **David**.

David *presses send. The machine starts to whirr. As the* Red Flag *swells outside, the page begins to feed, inch by inch through . . .*

Transition scenes 4–5

Rattling backwards now . . .

The funeral of John Smith, with the shocked Labour shadow cabinet in attendance – back to the election of John Smith as leader of the Labour Party, a 'new hope' – the resignation of Neil Kinnock – John Major triumphant in Downing Street, despite expectations – the 1992 General Election campaign – the Sheffield rally – the echoes of 'We're all right. We all right. WE'RE ALL RIGHT . . .!'

Scene Five

November, 1990. Night / early hours of the morning.

David, *here now the youngest we'll see him. He stands in the middle of the deserted office, holding a box of his things. No computers, no mobile phones. Everything around him belongs to the former occupant.*

Elizabeth *comes in – or tries to, the door won't open.*

Elizabeth (*off*)   David?

David   Round the back.

Elizabeth (*off*)   What are you doing, let me in.

David   The door's stuck, I came in through the / back instead –

Elizabeth (*off*)   The door won't open, / why have you locked the door?

David   Yes I know, you – go down the side of the Chinese / next door, and –

Elizabeth (*off*)   Oh stop messing about, David, please –

David (*louder, losing it*)   Listen! You have to Go down the Side of the Chinese, and Round through the Back!

Elizabeth (*off*)   Oh, for the love of – . . .

David (*waits*)   Elizabeth?

Elizabeth (*already going*)   Ye-es! I'm going, Jesus . . .

David *looks around. Puts his box down.*

A phone starts ringing somewhere, muffled. **David** *looks around for it, trying to locate the sound going underneath a desk.*

Elizabeth (*entering from the back*)   Urh, don't ever make me do that again, smells horrendous back there. The bins are spilling over into . . .

She can't see him.

. . . David?

David (*hidden*)   I'm trying to find the –

Elizabeth *screams, grabbing a rosette as a weapon.*

David   Ah! What? What is it?

Elizabeth   Bloody hell! I nearly went for you then.

David (*at the rosette*)   What were you going to do, 'campaign me' to death?

Elizabeth   Don't push it, it's a been a long night, alright?

David   You make it sound like . . . yes, it has; a long and victorious and happy one. Yes? No? A Member of Parliament? Isn't that what we dreamed about.

Elizabeth   Doesn't look like one of my dreams . . .

David   Don't know what I'm meant to do with all Whittaker's old stuff. Like a time warp. Maybe it won't look so bad in the –

Elizabeth   What, cold light of day? It is the cold light of day, as good as. You don't really have to stay here, do you, isn't there anywhere –

David   The local party have a lease, it's –

Elizabeth   Get them to find somewhere else. Honestly, this –

David   Bridges, love. We're meant to be building them, not burning them. Anyway, it's on the high street.

Elizabeth   That's not a high street. Kensington is a high street. The Champs Élysées is a high street.

David   I'm not sure the Champs Élysées *is* a high- . . . you know, you couldn't tell from your tone of voice that you're 'pleased' for me. For us. We *won*, Liz.

Elizabeth   Oh David, a tub of cottage cheese would have won if it was the Labour candidate; this is 'the north'.

David   The 'north midlands'.

Elizabeth (*looking around*)   I guess it's only when you're actually here, looking at it. The drawing pins on the noticeboard, the sad carpet tiles. Just reality sinking in, I suppose. (*Looks at her watch.*) I was about to say I might go back to the house but then I remembered how depressing the bloody house is.

David   It'll be fine, we just . . . we just have to *be* here. Be part of the community, we're not tourists here any more.

Elizabeth   Of course not, last tourists to visit here were the bloody Normans.

She kicks some boxes about, sits.

How can they have put you up here, I thought you were a rising – what's it.

David   They've 'put me here' because this is a safe seat. This is what safe looks like, I'm afraid. Those are the streets, the colour of the bricks, the types of pubs and cafés, the drawing pins on the noticeboards and the tiles on the floor. This is safe.

Elizabeth   They also look like North London, and Manchester and even Leeds, I'd have taken fucking Leeds – we should have waited, there was no rush.

David   No, there was no rush for *you,* you're sorted, there was for me.

Elizabeth *sighs.*

David   Oh please, Elizabeth, don't –

Elizabeth   What?

David   – *sigh.* All / the time.

Elizabeth   I didn't sigh. That was just – all the hope leaving my body.

Sorry, I know what I sound like, I know this is a good thing, I won't be this grumpy after a sleep and a bath, I promise. I promise. Well done.

She goes to him and they kiss.

David   Now we know we're staying here, we can get somewhere – nicer. Do you know what £40,000 gets you up here? A palace. To grow up in, together. Could even start thinking about, maybe, / starting a – . . .

Elizabeth   OK look, I . . . look, just, let me get this out now.

A phone rings from somewhere hidden again.

David   Ssh, shit, where's that coming from, that could be –

Elizabeth   David, leave it.

David   Can you see it, am I going mad? How can I not find this phone?

Some shouting from around back, in Chinese.

Elizabeth   David, someone's shouting outside. It sounds Chinese, from next door. I left the gate open, he might come in.

David   He's allowed to come in. He's a constituent. Anyone is allowed to come in. Hello?!

Someone tries to come in through the front door.

Elizabeth   Oh Jesus, we're surrounded.

David (*to the front door*)   Hello? Sorry, you have to go round the back.

Elizabeth   David?

David (*at the door, still*)   We're having some issues with the, um –

Elizabeth (*quickly*)   David, let me just say this quickly, I don't think I can do this, working here with you, I'm sorry.

David   . . . You what?

Another push at the front door – someone's kicking it. **David** *spins back to it.*

David   I said, it won't open!

Jean *forces her way through the front door and breezes in at pace.*

Jean   Yeah it will, just needs a kick at the bottom.

David   How'd you do that?

Jean   And believe me, I feel your pain. Gave me no end of trouble. Something to do with winter, the damp getting into the wood and expanding, or something. My husband used to plane it – is that what I mean? Plane? When you – fssshh. Anyway, hello, don't mind me, I'm just here for some stuff. Jacket, shoes.

Elizabeth   Excuse me, you're here for – ?

Jean   Shoes and things, left over. Just pretend like I'm not here.

Elizabeth   I think you have the wrong place, this isn't a charity shop.

Jean   You what?

Elizabeth   It isn't a charity shop, you can't just come in and take things.

Jean (*beat*)   Oh, I thought that's what a, uh, 'constituency' office was? Like a sort of soup kitchen.

Elizabeth   No, it's – no, you –

Jean   What about my foot, it's swollen, can I get that seen to? I heard something about a surgery.

Elizabeth   Your foot?

Jean   I'm pulling your pisser, love, I know what this is. You're the new 'me'. Or I'm the old 'you'. Ey in more ways

than one. (*To* **David**.) You've done well, haven't yer. Look
at her.

Elizabeth   The old me?

Jean   Agent. Terry Whittaker's my husband, 'all this used to
be mine'.

David   Oh, well –

Jean   Like I say, I'm not here to stick my nose in, fresh start,
no hard feelings, and with the greatest of respect, good
riddance to the whole rotten business, I'm just here for my
emergency stash. I meant my belongings, not drugs. The
only coke I've ever had comes in a can and makes me piss
like a camel.

Pulls out a make-up bag, some shoes, a jacket from a drawer.

Here we are. I'll give you this one tip, duckie –

The phone rings.

Oh God, that's one thing I won't miss. 'The bells.' 'The
bells!'

(*Going.*) You should answer that, they get a right cob on if
they have to leave a message.

David   I would if I could find it.

Jean   S'in the filing cabinet, under my desk – oop (*Slaps her
hand.*), *your* desk, sorry; old habits. You need a key for that
drawer, it's in the key box, there.

David (*going, trying it*)   I can't open the key box.

Jean   No, you need a key.

David   There's a key *for* the key box?

Jean   Course there is. You don't want to keep that
unlocked, it's where all the keys are! That one's in my
drawer – Jesus, *your* drawer, sorry love.

She unlocks the key box, takes out a ball of keys, takes one of those keys and opens the filing cabinet under the desk, removing the phone handset – still ringing.

Jean (*about to answer*)   What's your name again? Sorry, I've forgotten.

David   David Lyons.

Jean (*answering*)   Office of David Lyons MP, good morning?

Whom may I say is calling, and what is it regarding?

One moment. (*To* **David**.) This is the most important button – 'mute'. A godsend. (*Presses it.*) Some snooty cow with a plum in her mouth called Cheryl.

David   Oh, yes, she works for me, she's –

Jean   Oh bugger, sorry, I'm sure she's lovely.

Elizabeth   She is, as it happens; a close friend.

David (*on the phone*)   Cheryl, yes, David. Yes, we've just got in. It's erm, well, there's – it's fine . . . (*Continues under the ensuing.*)

Jean (*to* **Elizabeth**)   Listen, here's a tip for you. An emergency bag with posh shoes and make-up, in case your 'MP' has to cancel something – which is nearly always – and *you* have to step in instead. (*With a jacket.*) Look at this, I call it my 'packet jacket', 'cause it cost a packet and I pack it wherever I go. See, right now, I'm just a normal housewife, popping down the shops, until (*Puts the jacket on.*) . . . Ta-dah. Respectable member of high society, good to go. Couple of marks on it, doesn't fit as well as it did, but as long as you can do this (*Twists her arms.*) then you're fine, aren't yer.

Elizabeth   It's very nice.

Jean   Well, tell you what, you have it. Honestly, I won't need it anymore, I'm moving on, aren't I.

Elizabeth   Oh no, really –

Jean   You'd have looked the bees knees in this at the count tonight, trust me. Oh, not that you won't have looked the part in whatever it was you did wear.

Elizabeth   This is what I wore.

Jean   And it is fucking lovely, my darling.

David (*phone down*)   Sorry, that was Cheryl, she'll run my – what's it, parliamentary assistant, in my Commons office.

Jean   Well I hope you get on with her – I'm sorry, I didn't catch your . . .?

Elizabeth   Elizabeth.

Jean   I hope you get on with her, Liz, because that there is the most important relationship in British politics. It's the glue that binds democracy, it's like –

David   It's blinking.

Jean   You're right, it's a blinking nightmare if you don't get on, honestly.

David   No, the light, on the phone, it's blinking.

Jean   Oh, that's the answer machine, you've got messages. That's the first thing I do, Liz – *did! (Slaps her hand.)* Check the answer machine every morning. Burst pipes, missing benefits, noisy neighbours, all the world's problems in one place. You'll soon discover though that the majority of casework is actually dogshit.

Elizabeth   You didn't enjoy it?

Jean   No, literally dogshit, that's what the majority of letters are about, to any MP, up and down the land, I'm serious, that's what British democracy is.

Elizabeth   'Dog shit.' Right. (*Pointedly at* **David**.) Frontline politics, at last, ey?

Jean   You'll be fine –

Elizabeth   Yes, well David and I, we're not sure what we're doing yet, it's –

Jean   You're –?

Elizabeth   We need to properly, erm, decide what we're –

Jean   Find your own system, course you do.

Some noise outside.

Elizabeth   Oh gosh, that man outside, he's been yelling something –

Jean   Oh, Jing? You'll like him, he gives you a discount.

Elizabeth   He sounds very cross.

Jean   No, that's just the language, very passionate.

Jean *marches towards the back door and bursts into loud, fluent Chinese as she yells outside. She and the offstage voice have a brief exchange.*

David   That was – impressive. Chinese, you –

Jean   Cantonese. And only the basics. Jing started teaching me after Terry got Shadow Employment, they had a summit, all these trips to Asia and I can't stand just pointing and shouting when I'm abroad.

Elizabeth   Whereas here you seem to have no problem.

Jean (*she gasps, impressed*)   She's a feisty one, isn't she?

Elizabeth   I was only joking.

Jean   You weren't, but I liked it. (*To* **David**.) Keep her, she'll get things done. Anyway, forgive the intrusion, I'm like a month-old milk now.

David   Jean?

Jean   I'm 'off'.

David   Was it –? It was Jean, wasn't it?

Elizabeth   Excuse me, is there a bathroom here?

Jean   Bathroom? Oh, you mean toilet. Yes that's upstairs next to Terry's office – oh my giddy aunt, I'm so sorry, I will stop doing it. *Your* office. It's actually just something of a store room at the moment, junk from the past, he tended just to work out here with me. Do you want any bog roll? I don't mean to enquire into the intimate details of your ablutionary habits, but if you're going to need in excess of a couple of sheets then we keep that in a little cupboard by the –

Elizabeth   I'll be fine. Thank you.

She goes upstairs.

Jean   Well. Best of British to you. (*Goes to leave again.*)

David   You're a member, the local party? Surprised our paths didn't cross during the campaign.

Jean   Well, you don't want the old pair sticking their noses in, do you.

David   Your husband –

Jean   Is very pleased you kept the seat red – though not that there was much chance of it going blue, a sausage sandwich could get in here if it was red.

David   Is he alright, though? He . . . my understanding was that that's why he, uh, stood down. Health. Erm, pneuno-moco- . . . I'm sorry.

Jean   Pneumoconiosis, I know. We just call it black lung. It's his . . . you know, breathing and things . . .

David   Miner?

Jean   No, it's very serious, actually –

David   No, I meant *miner,* as in miner, not *minor,* he was a –

Jean   I'm joking.

David   Jesus Christ.

Jean   Sorry. Gallows humour.

David   Have you explored any – I don't mean to pry. Any compensation.

Jean   Oh well . . . maybe. He's a proud bugger. And oy, don't presume to – I was standing where you are, six weeks ago, and I don't need advice on benefits and –

David   My wife specialises in that sort of – she's a lawyer, she works in that sort of, you know, field, if you –

Jean   We're fine. He's fine. Thank you.

David   Must be – difficult. Being replaced by someone from your *own* side.

Jean   No, that's the best way, a by-election. Terry gets to retire with dignity *and* we keep the seat red. Win-win.

Have to say I was surprised when you got picked though. I don't mean that in a bad way, just . . .

David   It's alright. I'm not naïve enough not to realise you all came under some pressure. From central office. To 'have' me.

Jean   Yeah but normally our lot round here don't give two hoots what the guys at the top say – if anything that normally makes them do the opposite.

David   Why?

Jean   Why? . . . You know why. Grassroots don't like where it's all going.

David   Where is it going?

Jean   It's going 'right'. Isn't it. And I mean the opposite of left, not the opposite of wrong.

David   I am from round here, by the way. Just to – I wasn't just plucked from –

Jean   Oh yeah? Where?

David   Born about fifteen minutes from here. Over by Crosswell.

Jean   Crosswell? That's the other side.

David   The – other side of what?

Jean   The border; that's South Yorkshire.

David   Why, where are you from?

Jean   Up on the Lammas estate, twenty years.

David   Lammas? That's further away than Crosswell, that's like a twenty-minute drive.

Jean   Well yeah, from here, who gives a shit about here? It's a *no*-minute drive from *my* house. I'm in the 'actual' constituency at least.

David   I'm just saying, I have 'roots' – more than you'd think. Went to the comp, Dad a joiner, Mum a machinist, yes Oxford, but scholarship – I was lucky. And I wanna help others be lucky.

Jean   Accent's gone, a little. And you don't look like – I mean this as a compliment – your average Labour man. I thought you were the Tory candidate when I first clocked you in the paper, with all your . . . all your . . .

David   Well, maybe the modern Labour man is allowed to wear a / nice –

Jean   Oh yes, I know, 'the future', I received the memo, don't worry.

David   I wonder if I might . . .

Elizabeth *comes back.*

Jean   Find it?

Elizabeth   Yes thank you.

David   Elizabeth, Jean's husband, he's involved in a, uh –

Jean   Oh, no, honestly –

David   – an industrial disease compensation case, I didn't know whether there was any advice you could offer.

Elizabeth   What is it?

Jean   . . . Pneumoconious.

Elizabeth   Well. Honestly? The first thing to do is plead ignorance – you did all you could as a company to protect your employees. And in my experience, most of the people who sue for this type of thing get very intimidated by the whole process, the longer you fight it, the more chance they'll eventually drop the case.

David   No, actually . . . Jean's husband *is* the employee, suing the company.

Elizabeth   Oh. Erm. I'm –

Jean   No, that's alright, love, don't worry, you've given me some good inside knowledge of the shit they're going to try and pull when we do, so thank you for that.

Anyway like I say, I wish you the very best. Enjoy –

David   Could you just hang on, Jean, for one minute?

(*To* **Elizabeth**.) I'm gonna stay here, a bit, get to grips with . . . so if you want to go back to the house, then . . .

Elizabeth   OK. Well, I'll . . . I'll see you back – 'home'. Then. It was nice to meet you. Jean.

Jean   You too, poppet. Good luck with it all.

Elizabeth *tries to open the door, but struggles.* **Jean** *yanks it open for her.*

She goes. Door closed. Beat.

Jean   May I make a polite observation about your wife. Lovely woman –

David   And?

Jean   Completely unsuitable for what lies ahead, just telling it how I see it, this is not the glamorous, exciting, jet-set life of Westminster, this is the shitty outpost.

David   She was only ever going to be sort of part-time. She'd be with me in London, Sundays to Wednesday, come here Wednesday night to catch up, I'd finish at the Commons and come here Thursday night –

Jean   'Catch up'? Running the constituency office isn't a part-time job, I barely managed *full* time. What about your kids, would they live London or here?

David   We, uh, don't have any, actually. Yet. Why, how many did – do *you* – have?

Jean   Five.

David   *Five?!*

Jean   Yeah, all boys.

David   You have five boys?

Jean   Yes and if you do want any, honestly, just take one of mine, please, I'm serious.

David   The local party. They're not going to support me, are they?

Jean   . . . I'm trying to think how to be diplomatic, I can't, no they're going to eat you alive.

David   . . . Would you consider . . . staying on, for a bit? With me?

Jean   With you? Here? No, sorry, I'm sure you're lovely, and all that, but – my husband –

David   I'm not asking for the next couple of decades, just the next couple of weeks. I know you're sceptical, like everyone else, but I'm here to . . . I am here to try doing things differently. You said it, this seat is safe, so why not?

And oy, to the outside world I'm actually the centre, I only look like I'm on the right from where you lot are because you're so far left here, the *centre*-left is the right to you.

Jean   You know nothing about me. And oy, my Terry, you lot down at Walworth Road called him a troublemaker, but why is representing the views of his local party causing trouble, sticking to his principles causing trouble?

David   Don't get me wrong, I love principles. My headteacher was one.

That was a joke, you can smile.

Jean   I know I can.

David   The party can win, next election. If we're brave enough. I'm not saying slaughter sacred cows, but at least herd them into line. You know like . . . 'Moooo-ve' them on a bit. (*Smiles.*)

Jean (*smiling back, in spite of herself*)   You're daft you, aren't you. Moooo-ve 'em where? And why, just to get 'power'? What if the sacred cows are right and you're wrong? No, I don't doubt you and your lot will probably get us into power soon, I'm just not sure you'll do anything with it.

David   Won't you miss it? Why did you come back today?

Jean   To get my stuff, smarty pants.

David   I knew Elizabeth wouldn't want to be here, deep down, that's fine. I've been asking round for someone but no one wants to know – they want me *out,* and the first sign of a cock up, my neck'll be on the block, deselection.

Jean   So you want an older sister to make the cool kids like yer? No, no.

David   To challenge me too; me challenge them, work up some exciting ideas.

Jean   So you can show off, to Neil and Robin and Gordon back home?

David   . . . to *help* people. It might even be fun.

Beat. **Jean** *dumps her bag.*

Jean   Alright, let's get one thing straight, I'll help you out but only until I find another job, with my Terry being off ill now, I won't risk putting my boys out on the street, but once you know which is your arse and which is your elbow, I find another job, I'm gone. And I don't want you talking down to me with your Cambridge crap.

David   Oxford.

Jean   You want to know where I went?

David   Uh let me guess, 'the school of life'.

Jean (*hits him gently with paper*)   Open University. One of the great Labour inventions – when Labour *was* Labour. Politics, Philosophy and Economics.

David   Me too.

Jean   First class.

David   Me – . . . mm, well –

Jean   So you listen hard, take notes, and serve your bloody community from now on, and not just your paymasters at the top.

David   I'm pretty sure I can do both. But yes. Right.

Jean   . . . No airs and graces.

David   None,

Jean   . . . Alright. I'll put the kettle on. How do you take your tea?

David   I drink coffee.

Jean   For fuck's sake.

Blackout.

Act Two

Scene One

November, 1990.

Later in the same day in Act One, Scene Five.

Through the darkness flickers a TV image – footage of Margaret Thatcher, teary-eyed, on the steps of Number 10. 'We're leaving Downing Street, for the last time, after eleven and a half wonderful years, and we're very happy that we leave the United Kingdom in a very, very much better state than when we came here . . .'

Jean *and* **David** *sit on the desk watching the images flicker on the television.*

David   Do you reckon this might bump my bi-election victory down the news cycle just a touch?

I can't believe she's *gone*. I feel like this calls for a few, I dunno, dignified words of –

Jean   YEEEEAHHH – GOODFUCKINGRIDDANCE, you . . . you!

David   Jean? Jesus –

She leaps up to her feet giving the TV a series of fingers, pacing round.

Jean   Eleven years, eleven years, that cow has been . . . tearing the heart out of this . . .

She stops, leaning on the desk, gathering herself.

Sorry. I'm fine.

David   What does this mean, do you think? For us?

Jean   Open that drawer.

David *opens it.*

Jean   Take out my crystal ball.

David There isn't – (*Closes it.*) Very funny.

Jean It doesn't mean anything or nothing, it just 'is'. Tory party politics. Posh squirrels fighting in a bag.

David I think it represents a new opportunity / to –

Jean Let's stop wasting time, you're not getting any younger or smarter and I have a new life to get up and running, so – 'Being A Constituency MP', lesson one.

David Oh, OK, er I didn't know whether we'd be thinking more 'global' first before the nitty/ gritty –

Jean *Rule* Number One. The constituents . . . are you writing this down, I'm going to be going like the clappers, here.

David Uh, righ- . . . yea- . . . OK.

Jean The constituents are always . . .?

David . . . right?

Jean Cunts.

David (*pen down*)   I'm not putting that down.

Jean It's nothing personal. You're a cunt. I'm a cunt. Your wife's a cunt. When it comes to your home, your kids, their safety, your parents' health, your pensions or your benefits – we're cunts, because we have to be. When people march in here all cross and upset, it's because their family are backed into a corner and it's lashing out-time, that's all. I didn't literally mean you and I are actual cunts.

David Or my wife.

Jean (*not answering*)   So a certain amount of Buddhist like detachment has to be applied every morning when you listen to the answer machine, open the post, or greet them on the doorstep.

Because – there is no job description, there is no manual, there is no training to be an MP, you just have to start, and learn as you go.

Now, one of your weapons as an MP, one of your only weapons (*Dumping a ream of paper onto the desk.*), is this.

David   Paper.

Jean   House of Commons letter-headed paper, don't you know, it's almost literally the only thing that separates you from a normal person. Folk come here often as a last resort, having gone to every other agency and no one's helped. So *you* write a letter, to the councillor, school, GP, and it scares them into action. That's it. That's basically an MP.

At all the files of paper on the desk.

This mountain of death is your casework, letters from people, me and the other caseworkers can handle most of it – oh, it's up to you how many other people you hire by the way. Each MP gets the same budget for running their office and they can organise it how they like, so long as you record all expenditure and expenses.

David   And how many / staff do you think –?

Jean   I'll reply to most of this on your behalf; as far as 90 per cent of the constituents will ever know, I *am* you, I'll try to write in your – you know, 'voice', do you have a voice?

David   Course I have a voice. Oh, what, right, bland, centrist, managerial, you mean, no real distinctive –

Jean   No, not saying that. (*A large book.*) Constituency diary, Thursday night, Friday, Saturday if you want, we'll load it full of visits, fundraising events, press opps. We had our surgeries on a Friday, average maybe six people a week.

Outside of surgeries you have to build relationships with the community, headmasters, headmistresses, police chief, hospital trust. I'll get you started. Most important is the Leader of the District Council, that's Len Prior –

David   I know Len, he stood against me for selection, we debated at an All Member Meeting –

Jean   And he was favourite a'nall, until your cronies weighed in, so –

David   Not cron- . . . the NEC's By-election Selection Committee is / a democratically accountable –

Jean   So regardless, you should expect him to be combative at first.

David   Who did you vote for, incidentally?

Jean   You'll also need an account with the local newsagent for local papers, I cancelled Terry's subscription, but I'll set you up with another.

David   Your silence speaks volumes.

Jean   Most importantly – you Do Not neglect this office in favour of Westminster, I know you're there four days and here only Friday, but remember it's *this* office and the work you do *here* that gets you re-elected back *there*.

David   I should introduce you to Cheryl, next time you're in London –

Jean   London, why would I go to London? Fourth and final – all major votes in the Commons, you run by the local members here; you have to listen to them first, before the chief whip or the Leader or your own silly little conscience.

David   And aren't you forgetting the most important people? Who are our most important people, Jean?

Jean   Easy, the members.

David   No. The public. The *electorate*. See, isn't this is the problem? The, the cultish-ness, of Labour. Traditional Labour. The Militant rooting out non-true believers, it . . . it's just another Establishment, isn't it? End of the day, only on the left. A bully-boy club of Trotskyites and unions and it intimidates people.

Jean   Only because you're not in it.

David   I'm not talking about me, I'll take 'em on, I meant intimidates the most important people.

(*Searching, seeing the flipchart.*) Look, can I – this, can I use this?

Jean   Er, no you can't actually, that's mine and Terry's, it's where we'd do our working out – oy!

David (*drawing – a small square*)   This is the size of the party membership – what 600 round here? Couple hundred thousand nationwide. Very passionate and on the . . . I'm gonna say it, often the 'extremes', of the / political spectrum –

Jean   I'm not extreme / and I'm a member. Terry wasn't, isn't –

David   I'm not saying it's bad, it's obvious, when you're part of a club, any club, a, a trainspotter's club, you really like and care about trains, right? Whereas most people . . . (*Drawing a much bigger square.*) . . . don't, as much. These are people who normally vote Labour. People who don't care about the Labour constitution, are not involved in an ideological war, they just think we might be best for their families. This lot (*Voters.*) are generally a teeny bit to the Right of this lot (*Members.*). But they stick with us, regardless of feeling alienated by what this lot obsess about. Then . . . (*Drawing a much, much larger square.*) . . . there are these. The rest of the country. Tories. Liberals. Southerners, the middle classes. All to the Right of them. (*Voters.*) And A Lot to the right of *them*. (*Members.*)

Jean   Are you really trying to educate me on the political party I have been a member of since I was fourteen?

David   No, I'm – fourteen? You can't join at fourteen.

Jean   I lied about me age on the form, no one checks.

David   My point is that this lot (*Members.*) for eleven years – in *opposition*, I might add – Coincidence? – have been sucked into a bubble where they're convinced they have popular support, because when they gather in their meetings and sub-committees and sub-sub-committees, and propose to, to renationalise the weather, and everyone in their small meeting cheers, they think 'oh good, look, the world agrees with us'– not realising, or not caring, that *these* others *don't* agree. At all. But these members refuse to compromise in order to get into government and actually enact 'a *version*', yes, a moderated version, of their ideas, that is palatable to everyone, in order to actually make a difference to the people who really need them.

Well. My predecessors –

Jean   Do you mean my husband, the love/ of my life?

David   – they spent too much time thinking about this little group here.

Jean   Actually he devoted his *life* to his community and his principles, I don't care if that sounds soft, it is what it is. (*Grabbing her coat.*) And right now he's at home, with the boys, probably wondering where his wife is and I'm starting to wonder myself.

David   It's not about him, I meant – look, I know you think I've just been parachuted in from HQ, but I care about this, I feel it. I'm *one* of you, Jean.

I see two types of Labour people, all said and done. There's us lot; me, you and Terry.

Jean   Haha! / Right.

David   – Who come to the party – listen, with you 'haha-ing' – who come to the party based on our, what, life experience, class backgrounds, our local town. Right? And then there's a second type. Who come to it 'intellectually', who maybe find their leftism at uni, or moving to the big city, and that's great, all welcome, a broad church, we need Everyone. And my rival for selection, Len? – *your* choice – respectfully, he's the second group. And he says that me and 'my lot' are hijacking the party from you. And what *I'm* saying, is *they've* hijacked the party from *Us,* Jean. With their indulgent, academic experiment, dreamt up in, in the Islington living rooms of the likes of Foot and Benn, amongst their Marxist literature and Fabian texts –

Jean   I won't have a word said against Tony Benn, he sat on my chair once.

David   Fine! But you know who doesn't like him?!

At a 1987 electoral map on the wall – top half red, bottom half blue.

That lot, down there. Look at that. Red in the north, blue in the south. A country neatly split across the middle. What does that tell you?

Jean   People are stupid in the south?

David   It tells me that unless you make inroads down there, you can't ever win. This country, like it or not, is Conservative in its DNA, it's make-up, always has been. There are more of them than us, fact.

Jean   Not 'fact'.

David   There Are Not Enough Left Wing Voters In Britain. Not enough to elect a Labour government on their own, never has been.

Jean   You don't know that!

David   Oh OK so where?! Where is this hidden seam that hasn't been dug up yet?!

(*calms a little*) To win, we need every single one of our lot, and even then, we need to convert a significant enough Tories, in enough Tory constituencies, to get across the line. And to do that, you have to moderate. That's it. What other way is there?

Jean   You debate! Argue! Persuade! You tell them what you're going through, what they're *putting* you through, and win them around.

David   What, with Soviet-style, Marxist crap? How's that been going since 1979? Who are these 'great persuaders'? Fucking Hatton? Or Livingstone, and his, his North London, CND badge-wearing, cap-wearing 'comrades'. They aren't the Majority. It's just – *maths*. And, History. You win from the centre, always, that's it.

Every time, same bloody pattern, same lessons unlearnt – Labour lose power, the Hard Left enter, denounce the old Leadership for 'betrayal' of the 'values', and move the party to the Left, where we languish, in opposition, for years, until common sense returns, and we start edging back to power. Every time; 1951, after Attlee comes the Bevanites; opposition. Wilson arrives in the 60s, the centre; power again. 1979, the Bennites, and Foot, *opposition*. Finally, thankfully, Kinnock, moving back to the centre, creeping back to power. Because we have a leader who knows that 'compromise' is not a dirty word.

And. If you're someone who doesn't want to compromise to win, it's probably because you don't *need* Labour to win. Because your life is fine. And that is fucking selfish.

Jean   (*beat*) OK. I'll bite, clever clogs, so how *do* you 'convert' these southerners and middle classes and Tories; how?

David   By setting out a platform that pleases the most amount of people, for the most amount of time. Down the middle. Or what, I believe they call, democracy.

Jean   Or what others might call, a vacuum of any values whatsoever.

David   See, even this (*A poster.*), what is this?

Jean   S'the red flag.

David   What's it doing there? We changed it. Me, Neil and Peter, we –

Jean   Peter who?

David   Mandelson.

Jean   Him, oh I wouldn't trust him as far as I could throw him. Look at his tash.

David   So, what about it?

Jean   Well, what's he hiding?

David   His top lip? Look, a whole team of us began a journey towards something – 'new'. Baby steps. Beginning with rebranding, changing this, to a rose. A red rose. *Three* years ago.

Jean   Oh yeh, we ignored that. Anyway can't stand roses, soppy.

David   Do you know why we chose a rose for Labour?

Jean   Because it looks pretty but it's full of pricks?

David   Because – nice, by the way – because we *asked* people. We did Market Research, what people really want and think, God forbid, and then responded.

Jean   And this is exactly what the local party were scared of, David. That you're just a salesman, with nothing to sell.

David   Selling is important. And we are *shit* at it. And they are *brilliant.* Brand clarity and message discipline, these shouldn't be dirty words, it, we're . . .

(*Looking at the rose on the poster.*) Actually, perfect example, when I was working on this, I learnt – do you know the cultural history of the rose, as a symbol? For romance and –? It comes from the eighteenth century, as a code. A 'message', for lovers to communicate with each other about how they felt. When in a polite society, there just wasn't the – language. All those humungous and heartfelt and complicated, indescribable feelings! It isn't PR. It's communication. Talking. People just needed there to be a way to say – 'love'.

So I want to start communicating. And not just to the members. To the public. And I absolutely need your help. I need people like you, to protect me, from people like you.

And deep down . . . I think you could end up quite liking me.

Jean   Well it's been a long day, you're tired. And anyway what do you mean, 'like you'.

David   I don't mean like me like that, I just . . . think this could work. I do. Old school, new school.

I'm saying – help me, Jean. Stay with me, come on. (*With his hand out.*) Let's change the world.

Lights down.

Transition scenes 1–2

We move forward now.

David *learning to be a local MP – meeting the* **Police Chief** *for a photo. The* **Headmaster** *at the local school. Cutting ribbons. His Friday surgery with a* **Constituent**.

As behind him – moving forward – the images of Neil Kinnock resigning – the Labour leadership election in 1992 – the news of John Smith's death – the announcement for the 1994 election campaign, with Blair, Prescott and Beckett . . .

Throughout Act Two, older Labour figures, and moments from the past hundred years, can crash into the more modern images, giving a broader historical context, especially as we rattle towards the end . . .

Scene Two

July, 1994.

Brass band music, in the distance . . .

It's the night following the evening in Act One, Scene Four.

David *enters along with* **Jean** *and a young* **Margot** *as they help a limping* **Elizabeth** *inside, keeping the weight off a sprained ankle, clutching her high heels in one hand.*

Jean   There we go, easy does it.

Elizabeth   Ouch, ow, bloody hell it hurts.

Margot (*laughing innocently*)   You really went over, didn't you?

David   You should have worn those wellies, instead –

Elizabeth   Yes, thank you, David! For that retrospective advice!

Jean   Come on, feet up. (*Helping her down.*)

Elizabeth (*noticing* **David***'s eyes looking at the phone*)   It's alright, go on, check your precious messages, I'll live.

David   No I wasn't – just . . . (*He goes to the answer machine.*) Nothing anyway. Bloody hell, when you're not there you really *are* out of sight, out of mind, aren't you?

(*He sees his form sitting on the tray from Act One.*) Oh, that's – (*Screws it up.*) The leadership form, just – (*He puts it in a bin.*)

Margot (*looking around*)   God, where is this? Is this, like, where an MP lives, or . . .?

David   Oh, no, this is just our . . . Margot – was it? You fought really hard, for your dad, *all* dads, campaigning to keep it open. I'm sorry the result wasn't different; this bloody government.

Jean   Well, we're always on the lookout for help, Margot, you wanna chip in.

Margot   What, like, 'politics'. (*Laughing.*) I'm good,
thank you.

Jean   What, you don't think camping out in front of the
quarry every day for a month is politics, 'cause it is?

Margot   I just did that because . . . because who wouldn't
do that? You know?

Elizabeth   Where do you work?

Margot   Travel agents. Just down there.

Elizabeth   Travel agents, really? I was under the impression
people never left.

Margot   Oh yeah, Spain and things, in the school holidays.
Lanzarote a bit.

Elizabeth   Sell many one-way tickets, do you?

Margot   What do you mean?

Jean   Well, as I say, let us know, we always need
administrators, caseworkers.

Margot   I'm not a what's-it, 'member', though.

Jean   That's alright, folk just have to sign a little thing
saying they're 'sympathetic to the values of the Labour
Party'.

Margot   Sign a thing?

Elizabeth   In blood, yes, then there's no escape.

Margot   Am I sympathetic?

David (*at the TV – the remote control*)   Does this TV have
teletext or what? There must be news somewhere – oh, there
we go.

Margot   Well. Bye then . . . (*She exits.*)

Jean   No messages from the hospital either?

David   No – . . . oh, sorry. No. Do you . . . you could head off if –

Jean   No, the boys are with him, it's OK, I mean it – six is too many visitors, anyway, they told me he was fine.

David *nods. Paces.*

Jean   An emotional day. Tough. Seeing grown men . . . and all that.

David   Yeah. Well, best we can do now is get into government, get investment.

Jean (*beat*)   You're thinking about the vote aren't you – fuck's sake. What's it matter? You know your mate's going to win, but you've strengthened your base here by voting the way you did.

Elizabeth   Wouldn't it help his base to climb up the party ladder, though, Jean? Gain influence? He should have voted for the man who will *win*.

Jean   Elizabeth, the quarry *closed* today; hundreds of jobs and a hundred years of industry, come to an end. That matters to people –

Elizabeth   Don't say it like it doesn't matter to me. And if he's more powerful, he could have made it matter to *more* people, couldn't he?

David   'He', Jesus, I am right here you know.

Len Prior *returns, horn in hand.*

Len   Well. That's that, then. 'We've got to live, no matter how many skies have fallen.' D. H. Lawrence.

Jean   Come in, Len. Shall I get the kettle on? Or how about a whisky? David, do we have that – ?

David   Uh, yeah, somewhere.

Jean *fixes drinks in the kitchen.*

Elizabeth   David, are you ready, it's late. I'll get my stuff. (*Hobbling to the backroom.*)

David   Keep the weight off your foot –

Elizabeth   Well obviously.

David   Nice speech, Len. Very moving.

Len   Ah well. Moments like this, you feel the weight of history, don't you, the ghosts of – Morrison and Bevan, Attlee. Keir Hardy, even, all floating over you. All about to change now, though, of course.

David   What is?

Len   The party. New leader.

Jean/David   Who?

Len   . . . You don't know? Where've you been?

David   At the quarry, for the farewell, *with* you!

Len   I heard it in the car on the way home.

David   We walked! With – thanks for the lift by the way.

Elizabeth (*from upstairs, having heard, angrily*)   Oh, thanks for the lift, Len!

David   Who won?

Len   Blair.

A moment.

David   . . . Well. Well. I – I happen to think . . .

Beat. He can't help himself – thumping the desk in happiness.

YES! I happen to think that is BRILLIANT NEWS! Go on, my son. The final piece of the puzzle!

Elizabeth *comes back in.*

Elizabeth   It's Tony?

He nods. They cross to each other and hug.

Len   Oh well, we tried, Jean. Thank you anyway, David, for listening to our members. You did the right thing.

Elizabeth   Well, what choice does a person have, with the axe of de-selection forever hanging over their head?

David   Elizabeth . . .

Elizabeth   I'm sure David didn't become an elected representative to act as a mouthpiece for an unelected local clique – but anywho, never mind, David, table's booked for 9 pm, taxi's here in five.

Len   Whup. We know who's in charge now. Wha-tush. (*The 'whipped' noise, but without the physical mime.*)

David   'Wha-tush'? You didn't even do the . . . (*Mimes a whip.*) with your hand.

Len   The what?

David   Doesn't matt- . . . (*To* **Elizabeth**.) I'll grab my – from upstairs. (*Exits.*)

Elizabeth (*with a little phone book from her purse, at the landline*) We should try and call them, shouldn't we, congratulations.

Another phone rings. **Len** *opens his briefcase on the table and removes a massive mobile phone.*

Len (*answers*)   Hello?

Jean   Where you off to, anywhere nice?

Elizabeth   Just somewhere in town.

Jean   In town? We are in town.

Elizabeth   I mean, 'town' town, as in the city. The first person who *does* open a decent restaurant round here though, they'll make a killing.

Jean   I don't know, nearly 1,000 men just lost their jobs today, it might be a while till that sort of thing . . . you know.

Elizabeth   Yeah, no, I didn't mean . . .

Len (*has hung up the phone*)   Where's David.

Elizabeth   I do sort of . . . Jean, it does sort of irk me, when I say something perfectly innocently and you manage to respond in a way that makes me feel like I've just 'pissed on everyone's chips'.

Jean   I'm sorry?

Elizabeth   I know what happened here. I entirely comprehend its significance.

Jean   Yes, I know that.

Elizabeth   So . . . fine, nothing.

A horn beeps outside. **David** *returns.*

Elizabeth   That'll be our cab.

Len   David, who did you vote for again? (*Beat.*)

My brother. He said . . . he said he spoke to someone who said . . . the party register is recording that you didn't vote for John. Like what was asked.

Jean   . . . No, that's not – he did; that's a mistake. I saw him. David?

David *hesitates . . . A horn beeps outside.*

David   OK, look.

Jean   No. No. He wouldn't, he . . .

Elizabeth   Now look, look! David is the member of parliament, not you, you can't talk to him like that, like –

David   Elizabeth, just –

Elizabeth   Shut up a second, David –

David   Sorry.

Jean   Who did you vote for?

Elizabeth   Jean, with the greatest respect.

Jean   Oh, how is it when someone says to you 'with the greatest respect' you know they're about to really, really disrespect you, Liz?

A horn beeps outside. **Elizabeth** *moves toward the door.*

Elizabeth   We'll talk about this some other time. David?

David   Tell him we'll be out in a second.

Elizabeth   The meter will be running.

David   Tell him we'll be out in a second!

Elizabeth *sighs, opens the door.*

David   Look, both of you –

Elizabeth (*out*)   WE'LL BE OUT IN A SECOND! (*Slams the door closed.*)

Len   You faxed your vote?

Elizabeth   It's a 'her', if anyone cares. / The driver.

Len   You sent a fax? With your vote on? Jean, did he? Don't protect him –

Jean   I'm not protect- . . . screw you, Len, I'm –

David   Jean –

Jean   And screw you, too, David! If you *lied* to me, I can't / believe you'd –

Len   This button, here? This prints a copy of the last fax you sent. Did you know that?

A presses it. The fax machine starts whirring.

The fax comes out painfully slow. When it's finished, **Len** *tears it off and looks at it.*

And then looks at **David**.

David   Elizabeth, go wait in the taxi.

Elizabeth   David, they know you didn't vote for John, they have the fax.

Len (*with the fax*)   Actually this is a purchase order to Comet for a new washer-dryer. But, now we do know, yeah.

Elizabeth   I'll wait in the taxi. (*Makes to leave.*)

David   Washer, dryer?

Jean   . . . Oh that was me, I nipped back during the thing.

David   You're using the office fax for personal –?

Jean   Don't you get on your high horse with me, David Lyons! Not today!

Len   My brother has the form anyway. He said he'd send it through.

The fax machine churns into life as it begins to feed out.

It judders to a stop halfway through.

Beat. **Jean** *thumps it. And it whirs back into life.*

David   OK, look, we don't need to wait for the bloody – he's right, OK? I . . .

The fax landing in the tray. **Jean** *takes it.*

Jean   . . . 'Blair.'

Len (*hit the desk*)   You treacherous . . . You utter and total –

David   Sod you, Len! Jean, to you, I am sorry, I'm sorry that I lied, but –

Jean   I can't believe / I fell for it.

David   But why, why are you, are you both of you, incapable of seeing it?!

Len (*pulls his wallet from his pocket*)   Do you want to know what I see, David? Do you know what this is? (*He tosses a card down.*)

David (*looks*)   It's a Boots card.

Len   Oh, not that. Shit, I must have left – Jean, give me yours. Your card.

Jean   Len –

Len   Your membership card! Come on –

Jean (*going to her drawer*)   Oh my giddy aunt, I don't know where it is, do I!

David   What are you doing?

Len   You know what's on that card? On every membership card?

Jean (*from the drawer, handing a card to* **Len**)   Here.

Len (*taking it*)   You know what it says, on this?

David   Jean Whittaker, I'm guessing. Joined illegally when she was fourteen.

Len   No –

Elizabeth (*entering from outside*)   David – ?

David   One second –

Len (*reading*)   'To secure for the workers, by hand or by brain, / the full fruits of their industry and the most equitable distribution thereof –'

Elizabeth   What's he doing?

Len   '– that may be possible upon the basis of the common ownership of the means of production, distribution and exchange –'

Elizabeth   David?

David/Len/Jean   One second!

Elizabeth *exits.*

Len   Clause IV of the Labour constitution – the very soul of the party, since 1918, that links us *together* in solidarity! And you voted for the guy who'll tear it out.

David   For the guy who can *win* – because I actually *care* about the people you, you 'romanticise' about, here, as a little project. / I want to help them!

Len   Really, David, me, you're educating me on the founding principles of this party? A Fabian scholar, who –

David   Oh Len, Len –

Len   Jean, it's time, no more mucking about, it's time for him to go –

Elizabeth (*returning*)   Oy, that isn't your CHOICE! It's the *voters'* –

Len   No it's the *party's!*

Elizabeth   He increased his majority at the election, *again,* by *thousands;* how come a dozen odd members –

David   Jean, ignore him –

Elizabeth   – just because they pay a couple of quid in subs, think they have the right / to overturn the will of tens of thousands of local people?

Len   Jean, come on –

David   Jean, listen to me, please –

Jean   Oh, the pair of you! I'm sick of being in the middle, Christ!

David   I agree! The whole bloody country is sick of being in the middle of *this*.

Len   You're not the one at the council, David, deciding where the axe lands!

David   And you're not the one who has to come back to your town, after four general election losses – FOUR . . . and look your constituents in the eye and admit, admit, that you're powerless, to do anything, because for the Fourth, Fucking, Time in a row, you couldn't get your shit together. It wasn't the Tories closed that quarry, Len. It was us. You.

By refusing to bend, just a little, because of your fucking pride.

Len   Jean, you gonna say something?

Jean   What do you want me to say?

Len   I know what Terry would say, if he was here.

Jean   Well he's not here, is he, he's lying in hospital. That's our MP, there, whether we like it or not.

Len   Why you defending him?

Jean   Because he's my MP. And it's my job, regardless –

Len   Jesus Christ. The lot of yer . . .

He exits. A beat. **Jean** *starts clearing things from her desk.*

David   Oh, for . . . what you doing, Jean.

Jean   What d'you think? You still lied to me. You still bloody *lied* . . .

She gathers more things and exits into the back.

Elizabeth *and* **David** *are alone.*

Elizabeth   I can't bear it. This. I can't, these people, this life. Just get rid of her, David.

David   And replace her with who? She bloody wants to go, anyway, clearly –

Elizabeth   And maybe she's not the only one. You know I have options too. I have people wanting me to take up positions, leap at opportunities, not be chained to –

David   Oh how many ti- . . . ! We agreed on the path, Elizabeth!

Elizabeth   No we agreed on the *destination*. And it wasn't meant to *here!*

David   What did you expect! The keys to Downing Street in our first –

Elizabeth   No, course not. But I have a tolerance threshold. Like anyone else, like anyone would. And . . . and . . . and I don't know, and . . .

An impasse between them. The phone starts ringing. Beat. **David** *answers as* **Jean** *re-enters.*

David (*answers*)   Hello, can you just hold please? (*Listens . . .*)

Jean   Right, I've had a breather, I'm not going to leave you in the lurch, I'll work out my notice until you can find someone else.

David   Jean. It's the hospital. They say you need to go now.

Jean   . . . y- . . . I . . . I was going, I am going, tomorr- . . .

David   No. They . . . they say you need to go now, right now.

Jean   . . .

David   You're getting in our cab, we'll – Elizabeth, is it?

Elizabeth   Yes, course, it's outside –

Jean   Are they . . . is – can I have a word with them or . . .? (*At the phone.*)

She goes to it but wobbles on her feet, and **David** *holds her.*

David   It's OK, it's OK.

Elizabeth, I'm taking Jean –

Elizabeth   Yeah, no, go, please, go.

Jean   Oh God . . .

David   I know. I know, we'll get you there . . . Come on . . .

David *helps her out of the front door.* **Elizabeth** *is left alone. Watching them go.*

Transition scenes 2–3

Moving forward – **David** *breaks at a ceremony, watching the pit head come down – celebrating the victory in 1997 – at a council meeting pitching his plans for the new Data Centres at a council meeting . . .*

Meanwhile, nationwide – the Ecclestone affair, foot and mouth crisis, and the fuel protests – the 2001 election campaign – Labour being returned with a reduced majority.

Scene Three

June, 2001. Night.

A BBQ out the back door, winding to a close. **David**, **Jean** *and* **Margot** *with a couple of* **Party Workers**, *nipping in and out, drinking, listening to bad music . . .*

On TV is Tony Blair as **Len** *enters, in chef's hat and apron, holding BBQ tongues.*

Len   Right Comrades, we are Quite Literally cooking on gas out there now, three cast iron burners, propane fueled, with –

David (*at the TV*)   Cooking on gas here too, Len, look at that – first Labour leader to win a *second* term in any of our lifetimes, what do you make of that?

Jean   Speak for yourself, I was a girl with pigtails when Wilson won in '66.

David   This rate he'll get a third, never happened before in history, so.

Len (*clicking his tongue*)   Yes, alright, David.

Margot (*seeing the roses*)   Nice flowers, who they from?

Jean   We don't know. Thanks again for today, Margot, good to have a young councillor's endorsement. The 'youth' vote.

Margot   That's alright. No-brainer, if that investment really is coming, David –

Len   I might send an 'electronic mail' to our membership while I have a sec. Nice if they wake up with me in their inbox. If you pardon the double entendre.

Jean   You're pardoned. Because it wasn't really one.

Len   Use the computer upstairs, David – (*Before he can answer.*) ta so much.

David   Uh – be my guest.

Len *goes.* **David** *tops up* **Jean***'s glass.*

David   I think we have a New Labour convert.

Jean   Well. A ceasefire, at any road . . .

They sit. Drink. **Margot** *suddenly feeling like a gooseberry.*

Margot   Well, I'll go and see if my veggie burger's ready.

She exits outside. **David** *approaches the roses, swigging his drink. Sighing.*

Jean   I'm sorry, I know what it's like, that moment you realise, they're – that someone's not coming back. It's harder on the ones who are left.

David (*beat. Remembering*)   Oh God. I'm sorry, Jean. 'Terry' . . . today's date, that was really insensitive of me, I didn't even think, with everything. Sorry.

Jean   Oh shut up, I'm fine. Gets easier every year, you know.

David   . . . Does it?

Beat. **Jean** *shrugs. Smiles bravely. They look at the flowers.*

Jean   I don't know, losing a husband, it's like . . . it's just like one long, fucking *ache*. It doesn't fluctuate, or rise, or fall, or get better or worse, it just *is*. It's just there.

Are *you* 'OK'?

David   . . . I will be. Once I know where she is, what she's . . . just one way or the other, you know.

Still, 'the work goes on', ey, he Historic Mission, as Len would call it! Ey. (*Drinks, not believing it.*)

Jean   Funny, the language we use, still, isn't it, mission, struggle, a fight, even when we're in government. Like we're still the underdogs.

David   Well, I suppose that's because . . . we're the ones who want to change things. They're the ones who want to keep most things the same.

Jean What a glorious peace it must be, to be on the Right. To wake up every morning and look around and think – yeah, this is pretty much how it should be. This is fine. As opposed to knowing you'll never be finished. We'll never be done.

David 'It's hard to be Left.' Like you say.

Beat. **David** *watches her*

I'm sorry that . . . well, we don't really. 'Talk.' More. About life stuff, real stuff.

Jean Well, you're very busy, cabinet, what you've always wanted. S'good.

David What *is* going on for you? Away from . . . Are there any other . . . no other 'men'? On the scene. Or anything?

Jean Yeah, five of them.

David That aren't your sons.

Jean Please, when would I have time for that?

David Let's make time. Let me help you make time. You have to –

Jean . . . Oh, don't, imagine me, I haven't been on a first date since Callaghan was in office. And let me tell you about winters of discontent.

David They haven't 'changed' it, you know. Going out on dates. Love. One person, they look at another person, they feel something with that person they don't with another person, and . . . they tell them.

David *takes out a local newspaper.*

Look, you know what this is? A local paper. The Mansfield Chad. You know what they have? Dating ads. A good way to meet people outside the frigging Labour party.

Jean Why would I want to do that? I couldn't love anyone who wasn't a card carrying Labour member.

David (*looking*)   Come on, let's find you a Prince Charming.

Jean   Please, I'm no Cinderella. Although there's been plenty of nights I've come home with only one fucking shoe.

David   This guy, late 40s – a *barrister*, ooh. See, successful? Likes holidays in Italy, south of France, reading, films, looking for companionship, maybe more.

Jean (*taking it*)   He's obviously lying. (*Looking.*) All of these single people round here? Jesus. 'Accountant' – urh, kill me now. 'WLTM' – what does that mean? God, it's like a foreign language.

David   They're acronyms. WLTM, would like to meet. This one, LTR, long term relationship.

Jean   Why don't they just say that then?

David   Because they pay by the letter.

Jean   Well, I'm not going to go out with him then, am I? Cheapskate.

'Man, 50s, looking for younger woman' – I bet he is – 'Must have . . .'? What does that one mean, 'gas central heating'?

David (*looking*)   GS- . . . (*Sighs.*) Good Sense of Humour! Not gas – . . .

Jean   Look, I've got one man in my life who sucks me dry, mentally and emotionally, every day, and that's you.

David   I'm giving you permission to have a life.

Jean   I do! My boys, and – also, as it happens, I've joined an evening class, at the Fesi Hall, Writing. Sort of.

David   Writing?

Jean   Yes and it's not so ridiculous, got a good tradition round here, writers; Byron, at Newstead Abbey, Lawrence over in Eastwood. I mean, I'm not saying I'm them, but –

David   I know, sounds good. What do you do, just . . .

Jean We just . . . read, you know, and write, stories, and poetry, and stuff. Shit mostly. That's how I knew, about palindromes, and mirror poems earlier, where it means one thing one way, and something else in reverse.

David Like sitting the other side of a tram on your way home. Different view.

Jean Exactly. / 'Smart.'

David 'Smart.' But I'm not talking about classes, learning, I'm talking about going out, socialising with people.

Jean It is social, s'not just books, there's like – pottery and stuff, and – ay up, dancing. Dancing classes.

David Well, do a dancing class, go out dancing, meet people

Jean Well, look who's talking, 'meet people' . . .

. . . Alright, I will if you will; come.

David Me, you've met me.

Jean Yeh, don't I know it! I just mean you're always saying we should try harder, together, to – to get on. Well. We could do one. If you have time. The dancing class, thing. That might be one of the things we could – and then see cause it wouldn't be awkward, then, would it, having to – with no strangers.

David (*beat*) Uh, yeh, I mean, I could . . . although / I should –

Jean Unless you already can, in which case forget it, I don't want anyone making me look bad, I'm self conscious enough as it is.

David . . . No, no I'm not a . . . no alright yeah, that'd be fun.

Jean Yeah? Alright good. And don't show me up, with your two left feet – ey! About the only thing that is 'left' about you! Hah.

David   Aaaand she's back.

He downs his drink, and makes for the back.

Right, I need to go home. Need to – shower, or something, before they announce.

He exits, passing **Len** *coming the other way.*

Len   Right, that's done. (*Beat.*) Look very nice today, Jean, have to say.

Jean   Well, once every five years, have to scrub up, don't you.

Len   There *is* a card. (*The roses.*) There I can see it, fallen down.

Jean (*standing*)   No, I checked.

Len (*reaching in, pulling out a card from the flowers*)   Here.

Jean (*snatching for it, panicked*)   Give it.

Len (*laughing, moving away with it, reading*)   'To David. Some roses . . .

. . . for when you don't have the words.' (*He looks at* **Jean**.)

Jean   . . . He thinks there from his wife, ex, *almost* ex-wife, and he wants them to be, he doesn't want them to be from me, please don't tell him, honest –

David *comes back in, ready to go.*

David   Only had two taxis, Len, share with me? On their way.

(*Sees the card in* **Len's** *hand.*) What's that? Is that a card from the –? Give it.

Len   No. I mean, yeah. The roses. They're . . .

. . . they were from me. To Jean. Yeah. I was – embarrassed, sorry, I should have said.

Silence. **David's** *reaction unclear . . .*

David Oh. Well that's . . . that's *great!* Jean, what were we just talking about.

Jean Yeah. I mean, no, it's just . . . thank you, Len, that's very sweet.

A taxi beeps outside.

David Well. Er, why, why don't you two get that one. Go and talk, I don't want to be a blueberry, no raspberry, no –

Len Gooseberry.

David (*laughing – again, over-compensating?*) Gooseberry! Exactly, what's a raspberry? (*Blows a raspberry.*) That's one of them isn't it, haha. I don't know why, raspberries don't make that noise, do they? (*Blows another one.*) Anyway, I think I've made my point.

Go on, you two, I won't take no for answer. I'll see you at the count.

A moment. Them looking at each other. The taxi beeps outside.

Len Alright, uh. (*Shaking his hand.*) Well done again, David.

Jean (*desperate to stay*) I'll . . . er, I'll see you later.

David Jean? (*She looks – hopeful.*) Your roses.

Jean (*beat. Laughs, a bit too hard*) Oh yeah! Sorry. (*Grabs them.*) I'll see you then.

She leaves, closing the door behind her. **David** *is left alone.*

Margot *returns, holding two burgers.*

Margot So. Winning feels good, then? Does it?

David *looks.* **Margot** *offers her spare burger, as the music on the system swells . . .*

Blackout.

Transition scenes 3–4

David *breaks ground on the site of the new Data Centre –*

Nationwide – the twin towers fall – the war in Afghanistan, and across the Middle East – placards with Tony 'B-liar' – 2005 election, reduced majority – Gordon Brown entering Downing Street – the expenses scandal – Labour leaving power in 2010 – austerity begins to bite.

Scene Four

January, 2011.

A couple of hours following the meeting with **Shen**.

David *sits at the desk. He has a box of belongings out. A bottle of whisky on the go.*

Jean *stands holding a restaurant doggie bag, facing him.*

David   What are you doing here, thought you went home, to Len –

Jean   I dropped by the chippy next door, I saw the light on.

You spoke to the *Telegraph* woman. What's happened, how bad is it? What did you claim for you shouldn't've?

David   I'm not even sure I 'shouldn't' have, according to the rules, it just doesn't 'look good', that's all, it makes me look –

Jean   What did you claim for?

David   A bath plug.

Jean   A *bath plug?* They're publishing a story about a bath plug. So what?

David   It cost forty-nine pounds.

Jean   FORTY-NINE POUNDS!

David   It's – listen.

Jean   You daft bastard.

David   Er, excuse me –

Jean   Forty-nine pounds, of the taxpayer's money, on a bath plug! You need to give your head a good wobble, David Lyons.

David   It was for Elizabeth –

Jean   Oh, even better!

David   The new flat in London, back in – 2000 or
something; she was there the first night, I was, up here;
she wanted a bath, there was no plug, so, so, she went to the
only place that was still open, at 9 pm, in . . . (*Sighs.*)
Knightsbridge . . .

Jean   Why was it £49?

David   Well – hah, you're going to laugh at this . . .

Jean   Am I?

David   . . . No. It was. Like, gold.

Jean   Gold!

David   Gold *plated*. She told Cheryl it was all they had left –

Jean   Oh, it was Cheryl who put it through, I might have
known.

She takes out her phone and starts dialling.

David   What else was she meant to do?

Jean   *Not* put it through on expenses.

David   I meant Elizabeth. She, she wanted a bath –

Jean   Voicemail. (*On the phone.*) Cheryl? Two words for you.
'Gold' . . . 'Bath' . . . 'Plu . . .'

David   Three –

Jean   That's three, isn't it. (*Dialling.*) Press one, to re-record.
Hello Cheryl, four words for you.

David   Four?

Jean   'Gold'

David   Right –

Jean   'Fucking'

David   Ah.

Jean   'Bath Plug'. Call me back, many thanks.

(*Hangs up.*) OK. OK. It's not your fault.

David   People losing their jobs. Benefits. Going hungry. A gold bath plug.

Jean (*beat. She sits*)   You need to eat, look, here, have one of these steak pies.

David   No, they're for you and Len –

Jean   He'll survive, don't argue. Look, yum.

(*At the box.*) What's all that?

David   Oh, nothing, just . . . old photos and things. Found in the store room out back. Remember when we said we'd clear that out, after Terry, and I've only been bloody adding to it.

Jean   Oh God, not feeling sorry for yourself, are you? Memory lane . . .

There's still hope. The plant might come here.

David   It's not.

Jean   It might –

David   Jean, it's not. Marcus at *The Sun,* someone leaked it to him, he just called. They're announcing on Monday. Zeebrugge. 'Zee-*bugger*' – is going to be *The Sun* headline, so brace yourself for that particular gem.

Jean   . . . Shit.

David   Could have been worse, they were ready with 'Gdansk very much'.

(*Beat.*) You were right, what you said. Everything I've done, we did. Decoration.

Jean   I was upset, it's more than that, just –

David (*on his phone*)   Casework now, look at it. Worse than anything we've ever – in twenty years. That's how much a difference it made. (*Scrolling through.*) DLA benefits frozen, fella with spina bifida told he's fit to work, fella can't get his dad into a care home, nuther one no care home places, mum no school places, 'why is the library closing?' Sanctions on job seekers, food banks, food banks, son can't get a job, no jobs . . .

Most of the subject headings, in an MP's inbox, you know what they say – ?

Jean   Course I know, I'm the one opens them. They just say . . . 'Help'.

A moment . . .

David   When we had the chance, you're right, we weren't radical enough, bold enough. I wasn't . . .

Jean   You wanted to get in, *stay* in, it's – a fine line –

David   No it was a waste, everyone's right. CLP should de-select me.

Jean   Oh, I wish I had that gold plated bath plug with me now, I'd shove it in your gob. We're going to get through this. We going to up our game.

(*Lifts both their plates.*) See? Look, what am I doing.

David   What?

Jean   'Raising the steaks.'

Steak pies . . .

David *smiles, in spite of himself. And* **Jean** *smiles back . . .*

David   . . . Honestly, no one else can . . .

Jean   What? (*Waits, but gets no answer.*)

Do you want a hug or anything?

David   We don't hug.

Jean   No. Do you know what we do do, though?

She goes to an iPod dock and plays. **Jean** *holds out her hand, and he smiles, going to her reluctantly.*

David   Sorry I missed it last week, what is this?

Jean   Just a waltz, we'll go slow. You don't mind me leading?

David   Never, Jean.

They dance, turning for a bit.

David   You were very cross.

Jean   So were you. You look ugly when you shout, should stop it. You lose that handsome, like, twinkle in your eyes, and you go all . . . dunno.

David   . . . So you're not going to go, then, if the local party tries to oust me. If Margot does stands?

Jean   Oh look course, I'm not leaving, I was just upset.

David   Is that because you can't leave the party, or you can't leave me?

Len *knocks and enters.*

Len   Hullo. Thought I'd send out the search party.

David   I'm sorry, Len, I kidnapped your wife.

Jean   No, it's me, I'm sorry, David was in a bit of a – and so I –

Len   It's alright, I get it.

Jean (*wrapping up the food*)   Look, we've hardly touched it, just wait there, I'm going for a wee and I'll be back and we'll go, OK?

She runs out. A moment. **Len** *comes further in.*

Len   Sorry about today. Not being there, for the Chinese. It's . . . complicated.

David   . . . Sure, Len.

Beat. **Len** *takes a look inside* **David**'s *box. Takes out some photos.*

Len   What are these? Is that university? Oh, you acted? You were in shows?

David   Oh, no, well, sort of, I try to keep it . . . I don't like to –

Len   Blimey, is this you . . . tap dancing? I thought you couldn't dance.

In fact, wasn't that the point of all those hours, week after week, with Jean? The learning of . . . (*Beat. Flicking through photos.*) Because you told her you couldn't . . ..

David   . . .

They look at each other. Unsure. **Len** *puts photos back in the box.*

David   OK, it's not um . . .

Len   What? What is it not?

David   It was actually just because she wanted to / do something as –

Len   Do you know what, it's *me*, David.

David   Yes, I know she loves you, that's what I'm saying –

Len   I mean the coup. I'm behind the coup, it isn't Margot, I want you out. I've wanted you out since the day I met you. The day you came back to this town.

(*Aware of* **Jean** *upstairs, quietly.*) It should be me. This . . . should be *me*. I'm 'real', you're a – a 'nothing', always have been, this is *mine*.

David   . . . You actual bastard.

Len   You Red Tory cunt.

Get out – of my party.

David . . . She doesn't know? Jean? That you're plotting away to remove –

Len Jean has this warped sense of loyalty towards you, but she'll come round. Three of the key officers on board with me, I just need one more for a majority –

David . . . Well, I'll tell. I'm telling her, she won't go / along with it –

Len You won't, David –

David Jean!

Len (*hissing*) Wait! (*He produces his iPhone.*)

Jean (*from upstairs*) Just a second up, will yer, I'm pissing!

David *looks at the iPhone, confused.*

Len I was there. At the council today. When you 'rang', could hardly believe it actually. Played it back a couple times, I *recorded* it, modern technology, ey?

He plays the recording. We hear the answer machine message **David** *left in Act One.* 'Sahill. David Lyons. Sorry to call on a Saturday, but you called me, yer bastard. Anyway, Jean Whittaker . . . uh, look. I would say – I would say 'no'. Actually. I don't think you should take her on. She's . . . her heart's in the right place. But . . . I would personally look elsewhere.'

Len *presses stop. Smiling at* **David**.

David . . . That's not actually what it sounds like –

Len You aren't going to tell her. Because if you do, you will lose her.

David She should know who she's really married to, a little snake –

Len She's married to the next MP. And if the party aren't smart enough to deselect I'll just stand anyway, an independent, next time, and the next, and the next.

David (*trying not to lose it, starting to pace . . .*)   God, you could never quite bear it, could you, that I was actually part of the wave that *won,* that Got Us In, not part of your narrative, is it, the outsiders, the plucky anti-establishment protest / party, well –

Len   Where you did nothing but / damage the movement, and the party that I love –

David   – yes, I know. (*Louder now, not caring, pacing around.*) YES, it should have been better, but why can't you be *man* enough to champion the things we – like I don't know! Lifting millions out of poverty! Record investment in hospitals, schools, police! Civil partnerships! Tax credits! Instead of you / constantly sabotaging –

Len   Yes and the hundreds of thousands of dead Iraqi civilians, the –

David   Which I voted against! Which I lost my cabinet role for! / ANOTHER thing that you have NEVER –

Jean *has returned* –

Jean   Oh no, God! You two, honestly! You're like fucking children!

David   Your side doesn't have a monopoly on caring, you know, Len, on – on loving the thing we – (*Half at* **Jean***, accidentally.*) that we both care about. I happen to care a great deal, have given up nearly everything because of it. Right? So don't talk to me like I'm just, just PASSING THROUGH! After one marriage and twenty-one years!

A moment – **David** *having lost it maybe more than he had meant . . .*

Len   . . . OK. Alright, OK. (*To* **Jean***.*) I'm sorry, love. Just a little . . . exchange of ideas. In the very best tradition of, of Gaitskellites versus Bevanites. Multilateralist versus unilateralists. Healey against the Bennites. All in good faith, all . . . all good fun.

He attempts a smile at **David,** *offering his hand.* **David,**
reluctantly, **Jean** *watching, takes it.*

Len   Shall we? (*Heading out.* **Jean** *slowly following*).

David   . . . Je . . . Jean?

Jean (*turning, perhaps hopefully*)   What?

Len   Jean, come on.

Len *heads out through the door.* **Jean** *hovering back, looking
at* **David.**

Jean   You shouldn't think so badly of him, honestly, he is a
good man, really, and he does . . . he does care about . . .

. . . yeah?

Beat. **David** *nods. She smiles and kisses him on the cheek,
before leaving.*

He's alone, for a moment.

Blackout.

Transition scenes 4–5

Locally, the deep cuts in services – food banks – **David** *stands as the Labour candidate,* **Len** *as an Independent, in 2015 –* **David** *survives, just, his majority annihilated – Jeremy Corbyn elected Leader of the Labour Party – the EU referendum — the call of the 2017 election . . .*

Scene Five

June 9th, 2017.

Where we left off in Act One, Scene One – **Elizabeth** *and* **David** *facing each other.*

David   What did you say?

Elizabeth   I said I think I might want you back.

Silence.

David   I haven't seen you in . . . in . . . when did I last –?

Elizabeth   I'm sorry. I'm sorry, I thought they'd gone, those feelings, I thought it was over, but I just, I just –

David   When did I last *speak* to you, Elizabeth, when?

Elizabeth   Do you know how hard it's been? Being in a foreign country, alone, trying to make sense of it all.

David   Yes. A few percentage points *less* hard than it has been for me, given that you were the one who rejected me, given that I was the one who was *left*.

Elizabeth   Well, that's one way of looking at it, the other way was that you left *us*. The dream of us, what we had planned for, all those years, for . . . for *this*, to be here. It was meant to be a spring board, all those years ago, to Something Else, but then nothing, fucking – *sprung*. And you kept fucking getting *back* in here, and –!

David   So this has got nothing to do with me maybe losing my seat tonight?

Elizabeth   It's got everything to do with that. Did I ever pretend otherwise, was I ever not clear?

David   Just go, please, just –

Elizabeth   I'm not going anywhere.

David *marches over to the front door and opens it –*

David   Yes, you are –

– and almost in one seamless move as he opens it, **Jean** *sails in.*

Jean   Don't mind me.

David/Elizabeth   Jean!

Jean   Honestly, I wasn't listening, it was just genuinely good timing, I need to / pick up my –

Elizabeth   Please, Jean –

Jean   – my phone, I left it. (*Showing.*) Look, see? I'm going, I'm going alright. Look. I'm . . . I'm gone . . .

A hesitation – before she leaves the office closing the door behind her.

Elizabeth   It was never because I stopped loving you –

David   Oh! Do you know – do you not know how *unfair,* that is?

Elizabeth   I don't care! Life is unfair! This whole thing was unfair.

There's never been anyone else, you know. Anyone.

OK, there's been a couple of people, but it wasn't love.

David   Liz.

Elizabeth   *Elizabeth.*

David   Maybe we did talk about it as just a – a stage, on the way to something, but . . . maybe this is, actually, where I want to be. Maybe it is who I am.

Elizabeth (*incredulously*)   No, it *isn't.* It's just you giving up. You could have – could still, do something remarkable, we both could, together. Everyone always told us, we were going to go on and do amazing things together, they were fucking jealous of us, David. People *hated* us. And I *loved* that!

I know this isn't you, because I couldn't love that person.

David   Well then, 'hello', maybe you don't love me and never did.

(*Beat. At his watch.*)   It's – I have to –

Elizabeth   I came all this way. I travelled the . . . oh God, I must look a state. Do you have a mirror?

David   I – no, I mean yes, the bathroom, but –

Elizabeth (*going*)   Please. Please let's just breathe. And think about this . . .

She heads upstairs. **David** *alone.*

Jean *bursts in hard through the front door.*

Jean   RIGHT, YOU NASTY COW! You just –

David   Jean?

Jean   Where is she? That was –

David   She's –

Jean   That was my big entrance, I was working / up to it –

David   She's in the bathroom, and you can't call my / ex-wife a 'nasty' –

Jean   And what was all that, 'there's two Cambridges', 'two Yorks' – (*Shouting up towards upstairs.*) – YEAH NO SHIT!

David   Look, please, just – she's coming back, just go to the count.

Jean   She's only going to hurt you.

David   I won't let her. Please, I promise. I promise. I'll see you later. Just, go.

Beat. **Jean** *goes, closing the front door again.*

Elizabeth *returns from upstairs –*

Elizabeth   That was Jean, then?

David   She just forgot something.

Elizabeth   There was no towel to dry my hands. Some things don't change.

David   In the kitchen. But –

She exits into the back.

David   Liz, can you stop walking off, can we just –

Jean *bursts back in through the front door again* –

Jean   RIGHT, YOU NASTY – where is she now?!

David   JEAN stop trying to make an entrance! Just make a fucking exit!

Elizabeth (*re-entering*)   What's this?

Jean *does a quick open and shut of the door again, to get her 'slam' for effect.*

Jean   YOU! We're having this out, right? You don't see how much pain you leave behind, Liz. Because you weren't here, I was, I'm the one who's had to watch him get over you, not so you can waltz back and bring him crashing down again.

Elizabeth   Jean, do you think I don't see what this is? Do you think I've never seen? You're in love with him.

Jean   . . . *What?*!

David   Elizabeth. Please. Don't be so –

Elizabeth   You actually think one day, if you stick around long enough, if you make him dependent enough on you . . . that he might actually choose *you* –

David   Liz. Just *piss* off! (*Points at the door.*) Now, I mean it. You don't talk to her like that, you don't come in here and try and manipulate me like that, not anymore.

Beat. **Elizabeth** *goes to the door.*

Elizabeth   You're losing everything. You're going to be left with nothing, but you'd still rather *nothing*, here, over *something*, with me . . .

Beat. She opens the door, and leaves at speed.

Jean Da- . . .

David I ca- . . . I just, I can't, I'm sorry. Jean. I'm sorry. I just can't. I can't.

*He leaves the office, following **Elizabeth**, closing the door behind him.*

Silence.

Jean *gathers up some papers, with no real purpose. She stops.*

She finds the remote for the TV and turns it on. More confirmed results – Corbyn still in opposition, but with increased seats. 'What next for the Labour party?'

Jean *watches it for a bit before switching it off. She begins turning off lights around the office.*

The room slowly moving into darkness. The end . . .

*. . . **David** bursts back into the office through the front door.*

David RIGHT, NOW YOU LISTEN TO ME, JEAN WHITTAKER! We're going to have this out –

Jean (*a quick beat, before*) Don't you raise your voice at me, David Lyons!

David I want to know something.

Jean What?

David Why did you leave me? Why did you leave me, six years ago, to run *Len's* campaign, when you said you'd never leave.

Jean Why?!

David Yeah, why?!

Jean You're asking the wrong question, David, as per usual! You should be asking 'why did I come *back?'*

David I know why you came back, you left Len.

Jean   Then why aren't you asking why I *left* Len?! God, you're stupid.

David   I want to confess something, just a little thing, I don't even know why I lied, but I did. I *can* dance. There.

Jean   I know, we used to take those lessons for –

David   No, I mean I can really dance. Like I've always been able to dance. Like really. Like –

David *launches into a very accomplished tap dance, finishing with jazz hands, as* **Jean** *watches, bewildered. Beat . . .*

Jean   For fuck's sake!

They pace around in their own spaces, yelling louder than they mean to.

Jean   All those wasted – why didn't you tell me?!

David   Not 'wasted', and I never told anyone! The acting I did at uni – Tony had it as well. 'Oh he's just, he's just a performer, look at him, in his rock band', no substance, I didn't want to feed the –

Jean   You want to know why I left?! Because I *heard*. Len played me your little message, telling them not to give me that job. *That's* why. Because sod you, David Lyons. All these years, constantly sabotaging me but that one, that really hurt.

David   And you haven't been sabotaging me. I saw, on your little board.

(*Going to it, flipping the sheets over from the tally to . . .*) Mulling over standing against me too!

Jean   . . . You dick head. That's not what that meant! How did you find that?!

David   'David: twat. Little me, without future. Any view? Never. Could I stand? Under you? Can't, why? This. Admit, too scared. You are. Why?'

Jean   Or . . .?! What means one thing one way and the opposite the other? Like in the mirror poems I was learning?!

(*Jabbing at the board.*) 'Why – are – you – scared – too – admit – this? Why – can't – you – just – under – stand – I – could never view – any future – without me little TWAT *DAVID!*

Silence. **David** *staring.*

David   . . . How – the – *fuck* was I meant to work *that* out! Jesus –

Jean   You weren't meant to see it in the first place, not without me, it was going to be like a, a, a present. My way of telling you! Me finally finding the, the words. Wait, so *that's* why you told them not to take me at the council? Some petty –?

David   Oh for – that's really what you think?

Jean   Yes, I think deep down you can't stand me.

David   No, it's because I *wanted* you to STAND! To be my replacement . . .

Jean   Well . . . right, what?

David   If I lost. When I lost.

Jean   You're making that up, back peddling.

David (*marching to the desk*)   Right. Right. I'll show you. I'll show you.

He tries to open a drawer, it's locked, tries another, to find the keys to the key drawer –

GOD DAMMIT! Twenty-seven years and I still can't open these drawers!

Jean   Here.

She helps him. He watches her. She unlocks a drawer. He takes out a letter.

David   There. Constituency Labour Party, nomination papers, 2011. Jean Whittaker. All filled out.

She looks . . . doesn't know what to say . . .

Jean . . . Look where we are. We've come full circle, we're at war again, this party, the Left. Here. Everywhere. The different tribes. But for once, just once, instead of it being one side or the other, if we can forge an – I don't know, an alliance. Finally. Of all the vulnerable, the angry, all the hopefuls and all the left behinds, not *sides* –

Jean   . . . Me? What you talking about, me, no I can't do that –

David   I was wrong, Old Labour didn't hijack the party from me, New Labour didn't hijack it from them. We've *all* hijacked it – from *you*. The future . . . the *answer* . . . is you, Jean.

Jean   . . . Who's Eugene?

David   YOU! – JEAN!

Jean   Oh for – ! You need to fucking enunciate! No wonder we're always missing each other!

David   . . . So, is it . . . true? What you wrote? Backwards, not forwards. That you have . . . feelings?

Jean   Of course I have feelings. Everyone has *feelings*.

David   You know what I mean!

Jean   Of course I do! You mean do I have 'feelings for *you*'?!

David   Yes!

Jean   Right!

David   Well – do you?!

Jean   YES!

David   Right, then!

Jean   And what about you?!

David   Me?!

Jean   Yeah!

David   Yes, of course I have feelings for you!

Jean   Right! So why are we still shouting?!

David   I don't know!

Silence.

Jean   So . . . what then?

David   . . . Stand. Become the MP, you wrote the book on it.

Jean   There isn't a 'book' on it –

David   Exactly, so it can be anything we choose it to be, can't it –

Jean   And to what end? You couldn't fix the problems. And I've never known such problems as now; health crisis, care crisis, jobs crisis, Brexit crisis, crisis of confidence, crisis of trust, the country divided –

David   I know –

Jean   Never been a worse time to be an MP; Jesus David, I have to open letters with a glove these days; we've put a keypad on the door! A door that always used to be open.

David   Well if you gave it a good kick. So just – give it a good *kick*, Jean.

I'll drop leaflets through letterboxes for you, face off against angry trolls. Hold your umbrella while you stand at an old trestle table in the market square, flyering in the rain –

Jean   Look, I think we should just kiss.

David   . . . You do?

Jean   Yeah, I think we should just get it over with and see where we are, it's the elephant in the room.

David   OK well. Well, maybe we should, then.

Jean   Good, 'cause then we have to get going, you've got to go lose your seat.

David   Oh yeah. Busy night. Twenty-seven years . . .

Jean   I'm. I'm a bit older.

David   Not really.

Jean   I don't want you to . . . feel like you *have* to. I –

David   Jean, just shut up, for once, will you?

Jean   Don't you dare speak to me like that, David Lyons, or I swear you'll –!

He kisses her in mid flow.

Blackout.